PETRARCH

Modern Critical Views

Continued at back of book

Modern Critical Views

PETRARCH

Edited and with an introduction by
Harold Bloom
Sterling Professor of the Humanities
Yale University

CHELSEA HOUSE PUBLISHERS
New York ◊ Philadelphia

Printed and bound in the United States of America

10 9 8 7 6 5 4 3 2 1

∞ The paper used in this publication meets the minimum
requirements of the American National Standard for Permanence
of Paper for Printed Library Materials, Z39.48–1984.

Library of Congress Cataloging-in-Publication Data
Petrarch / edited and with an introduction by Harold Bloom.
    p. cm.—(Modern critical views)
   Bibliography: p.
   Includes index.
   Contents: Scipio vs. Laura / Aldo S. Bernardo—The ascent of
Mt. Ventoux and the crisis of allegory / Robert M. Durling—
The fig tree and the laurel / John Freccero—The Canzoniere and
the language of the self / Giuseppe Mazzotta—Negative stylistics
/ Marguerite Waller—Petrarch and the humanist hermeneutic /
Thomas M. Greene—Classical heritage and the Petrarchan self-
consciousness in the literary emergence óf the interior "I" / Aldo
Scaglione—The figure of the reader in Petrarch's Secretum /
Victoria Kahn.
   ISBN 1-55546-308-8
   1. Petrarca, Francesco, 1304–1374—Criticism and
interpretation. [1. Petrarch, 1304–1374—Criticism and
interpretation. 2. Italian literature—History and criticism.]
   I. Bloom, Harold. II. Series.
PQ4505.P4 1988
851'.1–dc19   87–17826
                                      CIP
                                       AC

Contents

Editor's Note

This book gathers together a representative selection of the best modern criticism available in English on the writings of Petrarch. The critical essays are reprinted here in the chronological order of their original publication. I am grateful to Patricia A. Phillippy for her assistance in editing this volume.

My introduction compares Dante's great "stony" sestina to the sestina by Petrarch it most strongly influenced, in order to suggest that Petrarch's deliberate idolatries are his crucial swerve away from Dante. Aldo S. Bernardo begins the chronological sequence of criticism with another contrast, this one between Scipio Africanus as Petrarch's epic subject and Laura as his more authentic, lyric subject.

The superb translator of Petrarch's lyric achievement, Robert M. Durling, ascends Mt. Ventoux with his poet in order to expound Petrarch's resolution of "the crisis of allegory." John Freccero, our foremost contemporary critic of Dante, reads Petrarch's modernist poetics in the context of the poetics of Dante and of St. Augustine's vision of the self.

Petrarch's revolution in the language of the self is expounded by Giuseppe Mazzotta, while Marguerite Waller reads the *Trionfi* as a grand instance of Petrarch's "negative stylistics" in his agon with literary history.

The Humanist mode of arriving at meaning, in an idealistic interweaving of the self's text and tradition, is argued by Thomas M. Greene as Petrarch's major way of interpretation. Another view of the emergence of Petrarch's authorial self out of the relation to the classical heritage is set forth by Aldo Scaglione. Our current concern with the problematics of "reading" is manifested in our final essay, Victoria Kahn's tracing of Petrarch's metaphor of "the reader" in his *Secretum*.

Introduction

Idolatry, however repugnant to an Augustinian moralist, is at the linguistic level the essence of poetic autonomy. Because language and desire are indistinguishable in a literary text, we may say that by accusing his persona of an idolatrous passion Petrarch was affirming his own autonomy as a poetic creator.

—JOHN FRECCERO

The anguish of contamination (or anxiety of influence) no longer seems to me a particularly modern (or Romantic) malady. Jeremiah the prophet shadows the poet of the Book of Job, Jesus Ben Sirach in his Ecclesiasticus is haunted by Ecclesiastes (Koheleth), and Aristophanes savagely mauls Euripides for his misprisions of Aeschylus. If we add Plato's agon with Homer, and the Gnostics' sense of belatedness in regard both to Plato and the Hebrew Bible, then we have a considerable catalog of ancient literary sorrows.

Petrarch's relation to Dante is enormously complex and difficult to judge, partly because Petrarch's own influence upon poetry after him was so great that it veils everything that is problematical in Petrarch's overwhelming originality. Each strong poet strives to make himself seem more different from his central precursor than he actually is, and Petrarch's strong misreading of Dante, implicit in Petrarch's own poetry, has affected us more than we can know, particularly in helping to present some among us with a Dante wholly given over to the allegory of the theologians, and so apparently altogether free of idolatrous or Petrarchan passion, at least in the *Commedia.* Here Robert M. Durling returns us to the deep affinities between Dante's *rime petrose* and Petrarch's *rime sparse:*

> To see one's experience in terms of myth is to see in the myth the possibility of the kind of allegorical meaning that was called

1

tropological. Petrarch knew and used freely the traditional allegorical interpretations of the Ovidian myths. But he dissociated
them from clear-cut moral judgments, and in this he was closer
to the Dante of the *petrose* than of the *Commedia*. To say that
falling in love and becoming a love poet is a transformation into
a laurel tree involves the sense that the channeling of the vital
energy of frustrated love into the sublimated, eternizing mode
of poetry has consequences not fully subject to conscious choice
or to moral judgment. For Petrarch the perfection of literary
form, which exists polished and unchanging on the page in a
kind of eternity, is achieved only at the cost of the poet's
natural life. His vitality must be metamorphosed into words,
and this process is profoundly ambiguous. If on the one hand
Petrarch subscribes to—even in a sense almost single-handedly
founds—the humanistic cult of literary immortality and glory,
on the other hand he has an acute awareness that writing
poetry involves a kind of death. This recognition has something
very modern about it; it gives a measure of the distance that
separates Petrarch from Dante, who gambled recklessly on the
authority his poem would have as a total integration. Petrarch
is always calling attention to the psychologically relative, even
suspect, origin of individual poems and thus of writing itself.
His hope is that ultimately the great theme of praise will
redeem even the egotism of the celebrant.

It is fascinating to me that one could substitute Rilke's name for
Petrarch's here, and still retain coherence, particularly if one also substituted Goethe for Dante. What Freccero calls an idolatrous passion (for
Laura, for poetry, for literary immortality and glory), Durling calls a kind
of death. Both critics are true to Petrarch, and to Rilke, or Yeats, or
Wallace Stevens, all of them in a profound sense still Petrarchans. Or
perhaps we could say that all of them, like Petrarch himself, come out of
the strongest of Dante's stony lyrics, the great sestina "To the Dim Light
and the Large Circle of Shade." I give it here in Dante Gabriel Rossetti's
piercing version, the best poem that Rossetti ever wrote:

> To the dim light and the large circle of shade
> I have clomb, and to the whitening of the hills,
> There where we see no colour in the grass.
> Natheless my longing loses not its green,

It has so taken root in the hard stone
Which talks and hears as though it were a lady.

Utterly frozen is this youthful lady,
Even as the snow that lies within the shade;
For she is no more moved than is the stone
By the sweet season which makes warm the hills
And alters them afresh from white to green,
Covering their sides again with flowers and grass.

When on her hair she sets a crown of grass
The thought has no more room for other lady,
Because she weaves the yellow with the green
So well that Love sits down there in the shade,—
Love who has shut me in among low hills
Faster than between walls of granite-stone.

She is more bright than is a precious stone;
The wound she gives may not be healed with grass:
I therefore have fled far o'er plains and hills
For refuge from so dangerous a lady;
But from her sunshine nothing can give shade,—
Not any hill, nor wall, nor summer-green.

A while ago, I saw her dressed in green,—
So fair, she might have wakened in a stone
This love which I do feel even for her shade;
And therefore, as one woos a graceful lady,
I wooed her in a field that was all grass
Girdled about with very lofty hills.

Yet shall the streams turn back and climb the hills
Before Love's flame in this damp wood and green
Burn, as it burns within a youthful lady,
For my sake, who would sleep away in stone
My life, or feed like beasts upon the grass,
Only to see her garments cast a shade.

How dark soe'er the hills throw out their shade,
Under her summer-green the beautiful lady
Covers it, like a stone covered in grass.

The Lady Pietra degli Scrovigni, sublimely hard-hearted, takes her
place with Shakespeare's Dark Lady of the Sonnets as a muse stimulating

one of the two greatest Western poets since Homer and the Bible to
unprecedented depths of imaginative degradation. Dante, already quester
if not yet pilgrim, climbs the high hills, presumably at twilight, or on a
winter day, in search of fulfillment, only to find that he is in love with a
Medusa. Petrarch's Laura, in one of her aspects, is also a Medusa who
transforms her poet into a stone man. Freccero and Durling agree that
Petrarch is properly ambivalent about being the object of such a transformation. The ironies of Dante doubtless transcend those of his son Petrarch,
but all the ironies of Dante's sestina seem directed against the poet himself,
and not against the superbly cruel Pietra, who reduces her lover to the
condition of Nebuchadnezzar, feeding like beasts upon the grass. Trouba-
dour love, culminating in the poetry of Arnaut Daniel, emphasized the
oxymoronic destructiveness of the obsessive image of the beloved that
the poet carried in his head. This is the disaster of a particular moment, the
precise time when the poet falls in love, akin to falling in battle. A purely
secularized moment so intense is bound to become a confrontation with
the Medusa. Here is Poem 30 of the *rime sparse,* a sestina in which
Petrarch has the courage to confront Dante's stony sestina:

> A youthful lady under a green laurel
> I saw, whiter and colder than snow
> not touched by the sun many and many years,
> and her speech and her lovely face and her locks
> pleased me so that I have her before my eyes
> and shall always have wherever I am, on slope or shore.
>
> Then my thoughts will have come to shore
> when green leaves are not to be found on a laurel;
> when I have a quiet heart and dry eyes
> we shall see the fire freeze, and burning snow;
> I have not so many hairs in these locks
> as I would be willing, in order to see that day, to wait years.
>
> But because time flies and the years flee
> and one arrives quickly at death
> either with dark or with white locks,
> I shall follow the shadow of that sweet laurel
> in the most ardent sun or through the snow,
> until the last day closes these eyes.
>
> There never have been seen such lovely eyes,
> either in our age or in the first years;

they melt me as the sun does the snow:
whence there comes forth a river of tears
that Love leads to the foot of the harsh laurel
that has branches of diamond and golden locks.

I fear I shall change my face and my locks
before she with true pity will show me her eyes,
my idol carved in living laurel;
for, if I do not err, today it is seven years
that I go sighing from shore to shore
night and day, in heat and in snow.

Inwardly fire, though outwardly white snow,
alone with these thoughts, with changed locks,
always weeping I shall go along every shore,
to make pity perhaps come into the eyes
of someone who will be born a thousand years from now—
if a well-tended laurel can live so long.

Gold and topaz in the sun above the snow
are vanquished by the golden locks next to those eyes
that lead my years so quickly to shore.

Durling's translation is prose, and attempts to be literal; Rossetti breaks through his own rhetorical sublimations and repressions in the impassioned verse of his Dante translations. Yet, without prejudice to Petrarch (or to Durling), a contrast of Dante's and Petrarch's Italian texts seems to me productive of results remarkably similar to a juxtaposition of Rossetti and Durling. I cannot conceive of a lyric poet more gifted at what I call "poetic misprision" than Petrarch; his sestina is a beautiful evasion of Dante's, yet an evasion whose gestures depend upon the stony sestina of the great precursor. The unifying element in those gestures is their striking and indeed audaciously deliberate idolatry, cunningly analyzed both by Durling and by Freccero. I wish to add to Durling and Freccero only the speculation that Petrarch's idolatrous gestures, here and elsewhere, are revisionary tropes, figures or ratios intended to widen the distance between Dante and Petrarch. In order to clear a space for his own art, Petrarch overtly takes the spiritual (and aesthetic) risk of substituting idolatry for typology, Laura for Beatrice.

Dante's sestina, if judged by the moral code of the *Commedia,* would condemn its poet to the Inferno, but then that is an overt power of the poem: this is the deep degradation of Dante before his conversion, before his turn (or return) to Beatrice. Still, poetically his degradation is Sublime, and can be said to mark a limit for the erotic Sublime. The obsessive force of his sestina is unmatched and is still productive in our century in poems like the sleepwalker's ballad of Lorca and the laments for barren passion of Yeats. Dante's sestina spares neither the Lady Pietra nor himself. She is stone, not flesh, and utterly frozen, as much a victim of the Medusa as the Medusa herself. You cannot flee from Pietra; her icy sunshine penetrates every covert place, and so allows no shade. She will not take fire for Dante as other ladies do, despite his hyperbolical devotion (or because of it?) and her lovely green is profoundly sinister, because it is the color of Dante's desire, and not nature's green at all. In some dark sense the Lady Pietra is antithetical to Beatrice, so that Dante's passion for her is decidedly idolatrous, anti-Augustinian, and a triumph for the allegory of the poets over the allegory of the theologians.

Petrarch memorializes the seventh anniversary of his falling in love with Laura, which he celebrates as a falling into idolatry, since it is also a falling into poetic strength. Fire indeed will freeze snow, snow burn, before Petrarch gives up poetry, since poetry alone allows him "to make pity perhaps come into the eyes / of someone who will be born a thousand years from now," a prophecy now two-thirds accomplished in time. All that is idolatrous enough, but Petrarch superbly culminates his sestina by giving scandal, by subverting Psalm 119, which in the Vulgate reads, "I have loved Your commandments above gold and topaz," to which Petrarch replies:

> Gold and topaz in the sun above the snow
> are vanquished by the golden locks next to those eyes
> that lead my years so quickly to shore.

The golden locks of Laura have replaced God's commandments, in a remarkable turn upon Dante's Pietra, whose "curling yellow mingles with the green / so beautifully that Love comes to stay in the shade there." Petrarch has won a victory over Dante's trope, but at the high cost of an idolatry beyond nearly all measure. Dante's response to Petrarch's sestina can be heard proleptically throughout the *Commedia,* which teaches us that what we behold must be the truth, since great or small we gaze into that mirror in which, before we think, we behold our thought. What Petrarch beholds is at once poetry, fame, and death; he does not behold a transcendental truth, or for that matter a demonic one. He asserts a limited authority, because after Dante's extraordinary authority no other sort could be persuasive or authentic. Dante, like Milton, casts a shadow of belatedness over those who come after. Petrarch, whose genius had to flourish just one generation later and whose own father had been a friend of Dante's, exiled from Florence with Dante, chose a gorgeous solipsism as his poetic stance. Call that solipsism idolatry or what you will; Petrarch urges you to do so. As a wager with mortality, such a stance invented lyric poetry as we continue to know it today.

ALDO S. BERNARDO

Scipio vs. Laura:
"From Young Leaves to Garlands"

Notwithstanding the fact that the last book of the *Africa* might give to the casual reader the impression of confusion and of considerable lack of cohesion, it contains much that serves to round out Petrarch's conception of Scipio. When the great Scipio says about himself, "Beauty moves my soul, and my heart, agitated by constant warfare, finds utmost solace in the sweet pleasures of soothing words" (ll. 74–77), we have the portrayal of the humanistic ideal of the supreme man of action acknowledging beauty, art and refinement. This moment precedes Ennius's exposition of the nature and purpose of poetry in which . . . Petrarch is conjured up as a reincarnation of the loftiest poetic tradition. As such, he will sing so worthily of Scipio that, like Scipio, he will merit the laurel crown. If we consider how Ennius's dream of Homer in the last book parallels Scipio's dream in book 1, and how in each case the central point seems to be the revelation of Petrarch's future role in the rightful celebration of Scipio's exploits, we detect not only a unifying device within the poem but a thematic strand of meaning which, in keeping with Ennius's definition of poetry, it is our responsibility to unravel.

In that first dream Scipio's father prophesies that only with the birth of Petrarch will Scipio find a worthy singer. In the last dream, the great Homer utters a similar prophecy to Scipio's favorite poet, adding that the as yet unborn Petrarch will be rewarded by a coronation on the Capitoline. This is followed by the double crowning of Scipio and Ennius.

At this point the reader senses a curious anomaly. While Scipio's

From *Petrarch, Scipio and the "Africa": The Birth of Humanism's Dream.* © 1962 by the Johns Hopkins University Press, Baltimore/London.

coronation, within the context of the *Africa,* is certainly warranted, the crowning of Ennius appears strange. He seems, indeed, to be rewarded for something he is yet to do, namely, a poem honoring Scipio. The reader cannot avoid recalling Petrarch's own anomalous coronation in 1341. As Wilkins has shown, Petrarch's poetic productivity was so slight prior to his coronation, that the basis for the unusual ceremony remains vague. However, there is little question that among the chief sources of Petrarch's desire for coronation was his love of Laura, whose very name was for Petrarch a reflection of the solemn implications of receiving a laurel crown on the Capitoline.

The final moments of the *Africa,* therefore, invite us not only to look back to the opening dream in which the focus is essentially on Scipio's unparalleled deeds but forward to Petrarch's own coronation with all its biographical echoes. This being the case, it would appear appropriate to examine briefly the manner in which Petrarch's other basic source of inspiration, Laura, seems to be related to Scipio as a poetic image.

When, in this same last book of the *Africa,* Homer, appearing in Ennius's dream, refers to Petrarch's overwhelming love of glory and of the laurel (ll. 229–41), the reader senses a strange fusing in Petrarch's mind of the images of Laura and Scipio as definitions of the loftiest human goals that man can attain. "Though late, he too will ascend your Capitoline in triumph ... he will restore ancient times with the eternal laurel as he descends attended by the Senate. Of all plants, the Delphic one alone will be dearest to him and he will learn to weave the young leaves into garlands" (ll. 237–45).

At this point, the reader also senses that this fusion, encompassing, as it does, not only the triumph of Scipio and Ennius on the Capitoline but also the reflections on poetry that echo all that is finest in the classical tradition, truly summarizes the total drama of Petrarch and his views as a man of letters—his lifelong dream of achieving in a literary work a fusion of the truths of philosophy, history, and poetry. This is perhaps best reflected in the very last verses of the *Africa* proper (preceding the interpolation concerning King Robert's death) where, as Scipio and Ennius descend the Capitoline following their triumph, Petrarch alludes to the many centuries that have elapsed and to his own daring attempt to scale the same heights in order not to render void the predictions of the "Greek bard" (ll. 390–409). What is most interesting here is the obvious similarity of the episode to the close of Petrarch's third eclogue where we see Laura herself allegorically crowning Petrarch atop the Capitoline!

It is not too difficult to find in Petrarch's writings other moments when the images of Scipio and Laura seem to fuse. In the middle of Petrarch's announcement of Laura's death as it appears in the well known notation in the Ambrosian Virgil, we find the following: "I have no doubt that her soul, as Seneca says of Scipio Africanus, has returned to heaven whence it came." But even more striking is the moment in the very early, perhaps pre-*Africa*, Sonnet 186 of the *Canzoniere* when Laura's literary apotheosis takes place in the same breath with Scipio's. In the sextet of the Sonnet, Scipio and Laura are chosen as subjects who, though more worthy of Homer and Virgil than Aeneas, Achilles, Ulysses, Augustus, and Agamemnon, had had to settle for singers of lesser note: Scipio for Ennius, and Laura for Petrarch.

> Quel fiore antico di vertuti e d'arme
>   come sembiante stella ebbe con questo
>   novo fior d'onestate e di bellezze!
> Ennio di quel cantò ruvido carme,
>   di quest 'altro io, ed o pur non molesto
>   gli sia il mio ingegno e'l mio lodar non sprezze!

[That ancient flower of virtue and arms, what a similar star he had with this new flower of chastity and beauty! Ennius sang of him an inelegant song, I of her; and ah! may my wit not displease her, may she not despise my praises!]
                    (ll. 9–14, trans. by R. Durling, *Petrarch's Lyric Poems*)

Both Scipio and Laura are here depicted as "flowers." Scipio was the "ancient flower of virtues and arms"; Laura "the new flower of beauty and goodness." But in the word, *novo,* as well as in the common destinies of the two figures, one senses a strong fusion of the two.

The image of Scipio receives further definition in three other significant moments in Petrarch's works, all three indicating some connection with or reminiscence of Laura. The first, already briefly alluded to, is to be found at the end of the third eclogue which once again discusses a subject very dear to Petrarch: the qualities needed to be worthy of the laurel. The interlocutors in the eclogue are Stupeus and Daphne, the budding poet and the demanding laurel. Early commentators agree that the eclogue is but another mise en scène between Petrarch and his image of Laura (as Daphne). After having convinced Daphne that he had truly been initiated into the sacred mysteries of the Muses, the poet is led up the Capitoline by Daphne who embarks upon a long panegyric on its majesty. Following a panoramic view of the glory dispensed atop the hill, Daphne's account seems to reach a climax as she points out that, "These were the heights revisited by that magnanimous youth, so long the object of your cares, who upon returning from the conquered lands of Lybia mounted here bearing an ivory staff (so great had become the renown of the place!) and accompanied by that elder [Ennius]" (ll. 152–55). The eclogue ends with Daphne crowning the deserving Stupeus. Once again we have, then, in this third eclogue, the allegorical representation of Laura initiating Petrarch into the exclusive circle of her devotees among whom Scipio occupied a conspicuous place.

But prior to the composition of this eclogue, which falls between 1345–47, Petrarch had rendered poetically a much more significant meeting between his beloved and his hero. In 1343 or 1344 Petrarch had composed his *Triumphus pudicitiae*. At the close of this Triumph, Laura's last earthly triumph before death, as she leads her followers to their ultimate destination, the Temple of Chastity in Rome, the penultimate stop of the procession is at Literno (ll. 163–77), the last abode of Scipio who joins the procession. At this point we see Scipio, the one "born only for triumphs and for empires" (l. 177) completing the image of Laura at the moment of her greatest earthly triumph.

Perhaps the most striking instance of the extent to which the images of Laura and Scipio merged in Petrarch's mind can be seen toward the beginning of book 3 of the *Secretum*. In keeping with Scipio's own advice as reported by Livy, Petrarch believed in modeling his life on past greats. His devotion to Scipio as a model was such that in this last book of the *Secretum* he actually has St. Augustine compare Petrarch's love of Laura to Hannibal's plaguing of Rome and of Scipio. Though the saint's implications are decidedly negative and he views the love with disfavor, Petrarch's reaction is of course the opposite. St. Augustine remarks:

> Oh, you fool! In such wise, then, for 16 years have you fed the flames of your mind with flattering and false images! That ancient and famous enemy certainly did not threaten Italy any longer, nor did Italy suffer more frequent violence of arms or more destructive fire, than you have suffered, in this age, the flames and assaults of a most violent passion. They finally found one who obliged that invader to flee; but who will ever disengage your Hannibal from your neck if you forbid him to leave and invite him in a servile manner to remain with you? But when those eyes . . . will be overcome by death . . . you will remember . . . your attachment with shame.

To which Petrarch answers, "The stars are not so averse to me as to disturb the order of nature with her death." Once again, then, we see Laura and Scipio as parts of a single image. Confirmation of this may be seen in another rebuttal that Petrarch directs to St. Augustine shortly thereafter on the same point. The saint had reminded Petrarch that Laura, like all mortal things, will pass away. Whereupon the poet answers:

> I have not, as you believe, fixed my mind on a mortal thing; and, furthermore, I want you to know that I have not loved her body as much as her soul, having found delight in those quali- ties that transcend the human condition and that revealed to me how one lives among the angels. So, when you asked me what I would do should she die an earlier death . . . I answer that I shall find consolation for my misery as did that most learned Roman, Lelius, by saying, "I loved her virtue, which has not perished."

The reference to Lelius refers, of course, to the friendship with Scipio.

Nor is this the only case of such a fusion occurring within a rhetorical device. There is a similar moment in the "Triumph of Chastity." Following Laura's decisive victory over Love, Cupid's state is compared to Hanni- bal's astonishment at having been defeated by a young Roman after so many mighty victories. Here again Scipio and Laura are conjoined in simile. Nor is it superfluous to observe at this point that at the end of this same Triumph when Laura stops at Literno to pick up Scipio, he goes along willingly, "nor did it displease him to follow a triumph that was not his own" (l. 175).

If we now attempt to make more explicit exactly what there was in Petrarch's concept of Scipio which made it parallel and at times fuse with his concept of Laura, the clearest answer seems to appear in still another work of Petrarch, one that was started at about the time of the *Secretum* and while Petrarch was still engrossed in the *De viris illustribus* and the *Africa*. It is the *Rerum memorandarum libri*, a work which perhaps better than any other reflects Petrarch's moral view of history. Petrarch appar- ently intended the work to be not only a detailed compendium of the cardinal virtues using widespread *exempla* from antiquity but also an exposition of the corresponding vices. This was in perfect accord with his definition of the work of a historian given above. The unfinished *Rerum memorandarum* was conceived of as a temple of virtues and opens with a book which represents what Petrarch calls the "vestibule." Here Petrarch establishes the necessary "preludes" to virtue: *otium, solitudo, studium,* and *doctrina.* Presiding over this vestibule, and consequently representing the model par excellence of the virtues, is Scipio, who is introduced with the words, "Who else could I, as an historian, select as standard bearer for this illustrious company than that supreme leader whom I chose to use for my poetic labors in the *Africa?*" (ll. 3–4). That this is indeed a place of honor can be gleaned from the fact that others of the immediate "company" include such past greats as Cicero, Augustus, Achilles, Socrates, and even King Robert. Just as noteworthy is the fact that Scipio figures most prominently in those books of the *Rerum memorandarum* entitled "De otio," and "De solertia." This would indicate that in Scipio Petrarch saw that blending of the active and the contemplative life which he considered so essential to the human condition. One may conclude, therefore, that not long after having set seriously to work on the *Africa,* Petrarch was conceiving of Scipio as the most perfect exemplar of the cardinal virtues offered by antiquity.

If, then, Scipio in Petrarch's mind is a figure of virtue and Laura a figure recalling on the one hand human beauty and passion, on the other human achievement and glory, the problem of why the two images have so great an affinity with one another is easily answered when we recall that a central concept occupying Petrarch at the very time all these key works were being written was that of the oneness of true glory and virtue. The two outstanding examples of this are the allegorical Canzone 119, in which Glory identifies Virtue as an elder sister saying:

> questa e me d'un seme,
> lei davanti e me poi, produsse un parto

[for she and I—she first, I later—were brought forth from one seed by one birth]

(ll. 74–75)

and the third book of the *Secretum* where St. Augustine admonishes Petrarch never to prefer the search for glory to that of virtue. He says, in part, "You know that glory is like a shadow of virtue . . . it can never be that wherever God shines, virtue does not produce glory. Thus whoever achieves true glory must also have acquired virtue."

The canzone also testifies to the strong similarity that Petrarch felt between the poetic images of glory and virtue. While Glory is called "Una donna più bella assai che 'l sole, e più lucente [A lady much more beautiful than the sun, and more bright]" (ll. 1–2), Virtue is called, by Glory herself, "Donna . . . che farà gli occhi tuoi via più felici [A lady . . .

who will make your eyes much more fortunate]" (ll. 59–60). And as
Petrarch turns to look at Virtue "in più riposto loco [to a more hidden
place]," he feels

> sì come 'l sol con suoi possenti rai
> fa subito sparire ogni altra stella,
> così par or men bella
> la vista mia cui maggior luce preme.

[as the sun with its powerful rays makes every other star
quickly disappear, thus the sight of me now appears less beautiful to one vanquished by a greater light.]

(ll. 69–72)

It might be well at this point to recall that both Scipio, in the *Africa,* and
Laura, in the *Canzoniere* and the *Triumphs,* are constantly depicted as
engulfed in light.

Of even greater interest is the manner in which the poem reveals how
Petrarch eventually succeeded in beholding not only Glory in her entirety
but her twin sister as well. He tells us that while he was "acerbo ancor
[still unripe]," Glory had made of him her follower. At that time, however,
she was in the habit of

> mostrandomi pur l'ombra o 'l velo o'panni
> talor di sé, ma 'l viso nascondendo.

[showing me only her shadow or her veil or her garment, but
hiding her face.]

(ll. 20–21)

Being young, he

> credendo
> verderne assai, tutta l'età mia nova
> passai contento.

[thinking I saw a great deal, passed all my young age happily.]
(ll. 22–24)

The day finally came when

> qual io non l'avea vista infin allora,
> mi si scoverse.

[such as I had never before seen her, she showed herself to me.]
(ll. 27–28)

She had granted him this revelation not only because he had desired her so consistently but because

> veggio che 'l gran desio
> pur d'onorato fin ti farà degno.

[I see that your great desire will make you worthy of an honorable goal.]

(ll. 56–57)

It is as a reward for this that she proceeds to reveal her sister to him and to crown him with the laurel.

In the *commiato* of the canzone the poet explains the obscurity of the poem in semiprophetic terms.

> Canzon; chi tua ragion chiamasse oscura,
> di': "Non ò cura," perchè tosto spero
> ch'altro messagio il vero
> farà in più chiara voce manifesto.

[Song, to whoever calls your speech obscure, say, "I do not care, for I hope that soon another messenger will make clear the truth with a clearer voice."]

(ll. 106–9)

In view of the fact that the great majority of the commentators agree that the "hidden message" of the poem refers to Petrarch's impending reception of the laureate crown as poet of the *Africa*, a Glory-Virtue, Laura-Scipio fusion begins to emerge.

In his perceptive discussion of Petrarch's concept of virtue, Theodor Mommsen explains Petrarch's reserve in making use of the story of the choice of Hercules as a tale extolling virtue by saying "it may be permissible to assume that he [Petrarch] was conscious of the fact that from the strictly Christian point of view, the story was somewhat problematic." In examining the two references made to Hercules' choice in the *De vita solitaria,* Mommsen concludes that Petrarch had not made more widespread use of the tale because of its non-Christian implications. In the second book of the *De vita solitaria,* it is stated that after "Hercules had spurned the way of *voluptas* and taken possession of the path of *virtus,* . . . he was raised to the apex of human glory." According to Mommsen, "Petrarch must have realized that to Lactantius, as well as to any other Christian thinker, 'human glory' represented merely a temporal good and certainly not that '*gloria* that cometh from God alone.' " Assuming that

Mommsen is correct in his explanation, it is, as we shall see, of particular significance that immediately following what Mommsen considers to be Petrarch's most revealing use of the tale (end of 2.13) Petrarch alludes to the virtue represented by the two Scipios, and particularly by the Elder.

According to Mommsen, the times in which he lived made it very difficult for Petrarch to define his concept of virtue in terms that would not go counter to Christian principles. In order to be acceptable, the concept had to include some link with the Christian interpretation of the eternal meaning of good and evil, and this was not easy with a concept having such a decidedly classical origin. Panofsky has shown that it was not until the fifteenth century that "the ancient concept of *virtus* as a state of perfection in this world was re-established to its full extent and at the same time reconciled with the Christian dogma." For Petrarch, instead, there was still a constant wavering between classical and medieval interpretations of the concept. Yet, "Petrarch anticipated that idea of the later humanists although he still conceived of it in a somewhat unsystematical fashion." Nevertheless, the fact remains

> that in his work *De viris illustribus* he never, either explicitly or implicitly, derived *virtus* from God. . . . Thus he provided no answer to the fundamental question as to who was ultimately responsible for the power which he considered the most important driving force in history. Through this omission he leaves his readers with the impression that he believed that a truly "illustrious" man, who by his own choice is possessed of *virtus,* is able to shape his own destiny, as well as being the maker of history. Such a conception was indeed highly secular and did not at all conform with the mediaeval tradition according to which all history is ruled over by God.

The general lines of Mommsen's argument are to an extent correct. The entire problem is, of course, a central ingredient of Petrarch's lifelong spiritual conflict and received its clearest definition at the end of the *Secretum* (Petrarch's examination of conscience) where, as we have seen, Petrarch admits a certain incongruity between earthly glory and ultimate salvation. But, in a way, there is also a strange resolution of the problem when he cries:

> I am becoming convinced that that glory which it is befitting to seek here ought to be sought while still here. The other greater one ought to be enjoyed in heaven where, whoever achieves it,

will not want even to think of the earthly one. I therefore think
that this is the order of things: that among mortals the first care
should be of mortal things; let eternal things succeed transitory
things, for progressing from these to those is most logical
whereas regressing from those to these is inconceivable.

This extreme position is immediately followed by a lengthy refutation
on the part of St. Augustine, but when Petrarch asks whether he is
to abandon earthly glory altogether, we once again get a surprise answer:
there is nothing wrong with glory if it follows virtue. And virtue, for St.
Augustine, is simply what, by the presence of God, distinguishes men from
beasts and keeps them from living a life dedicated to the satisfaction of
appetites. By dedicating himself to his books Petrarch is forgetting himself
and is placing glory above virtue. What he should do is to meditate on
death and the afterlife. But, as we have seen, Petrarch chooses to finish his
works first.

Some modifications in Mommsen's argument are therefore called for
if we consider Scipio as the exemplar who, better than Hercules or any
other figure, best personified Petrarch's concept of virtue. Indeed the very
passage following the Hercules reference in the *De vita solitaria* already
contains an attempt to fill the lacuna indicated by Mommsen. In it Petrarch
is supposedly demonstrating the role played by solitude in the lives of the
two Scipios, but in discussing their most praiseworthy qualities, it is the
religious and spiritual note that prevails:

> The first of these [the hero of the *Africa*], as Livy relates,
> "never at any time, from his first assumption of the manly
> gown, transacted any business, public or private, without first
> going to the Capitoline, entering the temple, and taking his seat
> there." This habit he retained all his life. That extraordinary
> man, then, celebrated not by the superstitious legends of the
> Greeks, but by the judgment of the Romans—he also because
> of his extraordinary virtue was considered of divine origin—
> took religion for the basis of all his actions. . . . With such a
> basis he would approach all undertakings with a superhuman
> confidence and promise himself and his followers the most
> prosperous outcome without ever failing to succeed. Moreover,
> . . . it is generally known that both [Scipios] . . . were as
> devoted to solitude as they were to virtue.

Worthy of particular note is the reference to the "legendary" and
"superstitious" nature of the lives and deeds of heroes such as Hercules,

Romulus, and Achilles (who had appeared in the preceding section) as compared to the truly historical accomplishments of Scipio. In fact, in writing that Hercules "scorning the way of pleasure in the end entered upon the path of virtue; and pursued it without tiring, succeeding thereby in achieving not only the apex of earthly glory but in being considered a god," and then turning his attention to Scipio, Petrarch seems to be turning from the realm of possible fancy to that of fact. That this historical orientation of the new humanist represented a radical departure from the traditional view of Hercules can be seen in the manner in which Hercules had been "adopted" by Christian writers from a very early date.

Of similar significance are the passages that follow in which he takes issue with St. Ambrose for having tried to attribute one of Scipio's famous sayings to the "prophets of the Lord, Moses, Elijah and Elisha." Though respectful of the authority of St. Ambrose, Petrarch argues in support of the view that it really was Scipio who pronounced the saying first. Nor is this the only occasion when Petrarch implies that Scipio possessed a wisdom not unworthy of biblical heroes. In book 2 of the *De otio religioso* a similar moment occurs, this time involving another phrase uttered by Scipio on the nature of sin. It is the warning that Scipio gives to Massinissa urging him not to spoil his numerous merits with "a degree of guilt more than proportioned to the value of its object." The statement gives rise to Petrarch's exclaiming:

> Oh remarkable words worthy, not so much of a young military leader, as of an elder or a lofty poet, or of a distinguished philosopher or even of an apostle! . . . Oh would that all those who are about to sin especially in lust would ponder and weigh these words, so that when the violent drive oppresses the flesh the excited mind may at least restrain itself with this rein.

Thus, while it may be true, as Mommsen says, that the tale of Hercules as used by Petrarch indicates an awareness by Petrarch of the irreconcilability of classical and Christian concepts of Virtue, it appears that in the figure of Scipio, Petrarch tried to portray a human glory and virtue which, harmonizing and coalescing, could even historically be said to have some association with the Christian heritage. We might even venture to say at this point that the *Africa* was inspired by a desire to provide the biography of Scipio as it appears in the *De viris* with those qualities which, while not directly Christian, are so in an oblique and mysterious fashion. Something similar can certainly be said in distinguishing between the Laura of the *Canzoniere* and the Laura of the *Triumphs*.

Interestingly enough, since the very beginning, one of the chief criticisms directed against the *Africa* was precisely this anachronistic use of
Christian motifs. This was, indeed, the principal objection levelled against
the only verses of the *Africa* presumably made public during Petrarch's
lifetime. It is worth noting the manner in which Petrarch defends himself
against such charges. In *Seniles* (2.1) written some ten years before his
death, he alludes to the "calumnies" suffered by "the thirty-four as yet
unpolished verses" of the Mago episode that he, for the sake of friendship,
had felt compelled to release to Barbato da Sulmone. Petrarch rather
vehemently refutes the accusation that the words he had put into the
mouth of the dying Mago were more befitting a Christian than a pagan.
What he says, in effect, is that there is a certain fund of ideas common to
men of all ages which reveal Man's inherent dignity, wisdom, and spirituality.
These ideas cannot be classified either as Christian or non-Christian, as
can be seen in the many examples adduced to prove the point. Therefore,
"the self-examination, the remorse of conscience, the repentance and the
confession" to be found in the Mago episode "are things common to all
men and nations."

The difficulties experienced by Petrarch in trying to make Scipio a
figure of virtue that would not be inconsistent with Christian values were
similar to those experienced in his attempts to define glory through the
image of Laura. In trying to reconcile his concept of glory with Christian
principles, Petrarch used the following argument, quoted in part above, in
his imagined discussion with St. Augustine in the last book of the *Secretum*. "I am not contemplating becoming a god in order to attain eternity
or to embrace heaven and earth. Human glory is sufficient for me; only
this do I long for, and, mortal that I am, I desire only mortal things." To
which the astonished saint answers: "Oh, unhappy man that you must be
if you tell the truth! If you do not desire things immortal, if you do not
long for things eternal, you are totally earthly. Your destiny is decided,
there is no hope left for you." It is at this point that Petrarch reaches an
ingenious compromise with the saint's position. "May God keep me from
such insanity! My conscience, mindful of my cares, is witness to the fact
that I have always burned with the love of eternal things. This is what I am
saying, or, if I expressed myself badly, this is what I meant to say: I use
mortal goods as mortal things, nor do I try to do violence to things of
nature with immoderate or enormous desires. I thus long for human glory
as one who knows that both he and it are mortal." This compromise is
acceptable to the saint, but since it is really referring to what Petrarch
hopes to gain through his works dealing with Scipio, it indicates an

attempt to justify what appears to be a basically non-Christian position in Christian terms.

That in the *Africa* Scipio is a model of the classical virtues of prudence, temperance, fortitude, and justice can hardly be denied. But, as a historian, Petrarch could never ascribe to Scipio the three Christian virtues of faith, hope, and charity. On the other hand, the poem does possess signs of a constant attempt by Petrarch to make Scipio either the instrument of a Christian Providence or the unconscious follower of the three Christian virtues. This was in keeping with the following passage of St. Paul's Epistle to the Romans which had also served Abailard in his defense of pagan philosophers: "The knowledge of God is clear to their minds; God himself has made it clear to them; from the foundations of the world men have caught sight of his invisible nature, his eternal power and divineness, as they are known through his creatures" (Rom. 1:19).

It can be said, therefore, that the *Africa* is an endeavor by Petrarch to write lofty poetry as he conceived it, a poetry partaking primarily of the classical, but with clear Christian overtones. It starts with human values and perfection, and stretches them to the maximum degree by projecting them on the screen of an indistinct Christian eternity in order to show what awaits men of virtue. As I have indicated in another study devoted to Petrarch's poetics:

> If a great poet could speak of human values in such a manner as to imply not only moral but spiritual ones, all the better. The ultimate purpose of the Christian poet, like that of the great ancients, is to promote virtue. But for Petrarch virtue consists of the ability to "recte sentire de Deo et recte inter homines agere" (*Fam.* 11.3). The three theological virtues must supplement the four cardinal virtues. Nonetheless, while the inference seems to be that all great poetry tends to *transumanar*, it must do so without breaking the link with the human, for the human partakes of the divine.

At the end of the *Africa* Scipio is assured of an enduring human glory in and beyond time as he stands atop the Capitoline united with Poetry as the savior of Rome, the eternal city that the Christian God Himself, as mysteriously revealed in book 7, intends someday to make his official abode on earth. At the end of the *Triumphs* there is a vision of the earthly Laura confidently heading a triumph beyond death, fame, and time to a "new world" recalling the Christian Paradise, but in human terms. In the *Secretum* while Petrarch begrudgingly admits that perhaps he is guilty of an excessive love of Laura, he clings tenaciously to the view that the works in which he was seeking to glorify "the illustrious Roman youth" were not dangerous to the welfare of his soul. This view, as we have seen, receives even greater emphasis in the first eclogue. In the *Canzoniere* also, those poems not dealing with Petrarch's love of Laura reveal either Petrarch's love of God or his love for a superior glory.

In the *Africa,* then, Scipio summarizes in Latin a humanistic ideal whose counterpart Petrarch had tried all his life to define in Italian through the image of Laura: a concept of virtue that complements a concept of glory in a way that makes both acquire near-Christian hues. In the two "epics" devoted to these two protagonists, the *Africa* and the *Triumphs* respectively, Petrarch sought to achieve a lifelong ambition which Umberto Bosco defines as follows, "Heaven and earth reconciled; this is the great, impossible dream of Petrarch's entire existence."

There is a great deal in common between the closing moments of the *Africa* and the closing moments of the "Triumph of Eternity." At the very end of the *Africa,* as Scipio returns to Rome with his victorious forces, all nature seems to rejoice: "The eye of the sun had never yet seen a day so beautiful in Italian skies. With her hair bedecked with roses, and her lovely, rosy face, Aurora yoked the fiery horses of Phoebus to the golden chariot, and Phoebus himself, gayer than usual, and much more hand-some, took hold the reins, and from the haughty peaks of the wooded Appenines directed his eager glance to Rome" (ll. 324–29). And as Scipio advances at the head of the long column through streets bedecked with "golden carpets . . . platforms laden with gems and purple velvet . . . and row upon row of huge pavilions," we see him "with serene countenance, upon a purple chariot, exalted, shining; and his eyes, his forehead, his bearing made him appear a heavenly thing, as he truly was. Four horses whiter than snow drew his chariot" (ll. 338–41). Bringing up the rear of the glorious triumph is the Roman Army in full battle dress. As it sets foot on the soil of Rome, "The victorious trumpets and every other instrument resounded in a loud, tremendous clamor. The waves of the Tiber were shaken, while near and far the forests trembled, as did the lofty walls. Waves of sound shook Alba . . . and vast Olympus, at the resounding of the lands, joined in" (ll. 382–86). Following appropriate rites to the deities atop the Capitoline, Scipio asks for himself only a lasting name, for "With his triumph over Hannibal he opened wide the road to future triumphs. . . . To be subject to Rome and to the Universe and to have as masters the sons of Quirinus . . . no people dared refuse, after Carthage wore the Roman yoke" (ll. 393–97). As the poem draws to a close, we see Scipio descending the hill on a chariot with the poet, Ennius, at his right, likewise wearing the laurel garland. Thus did Scipio establish not only the invincibility of Rome but also the lofty significance of the Roman triumph.

At the end of the "Triumph of Eternity" we find a similar scene, but here it is Laura who heads the greatest of all triumphs. When both Time and Death will be "dead," those most worthy of true glory "will receive eternal Glory with immortal beauty" (l. 134). But leading all these will be "she whom the weeping world calls with my voice and my weary pen; but whom heaven also desires to see entire" (ll. 136–38).

If we now turn, for a moment, to two preceding Triumphs, we find a curious rapport established between Scipio and Laura which sheds considerable light on the relationship between the "Triumph of Eternity" and the concluding moments of the *Africa*. We have already seen that Laura's last human triumph, that of Chastity, reaches a climax when she leads a kind of pilgrimage to Scipio's country retreat in order to receive him in her retinue. In the "Triumph of Glory" something very similar, and perhaps more significant, happens. Laura is dead, and in her place there steps another "bella donna." In the "Triumph of Death" Laura's departure had been, for Petrarch, an incident that had "extinguished the sun, indeed had returned it to the heavens, leaving me here like a blind man" (canto 2.2–3). Now, in the "Triumph of Glory," the new goddess appears as the planet Venus that precedes the sun at dawn. This is, of course, the proper position for Glory—the lesser of the two brightest heavenly lights—as revealed in Canzone 119. What is of particular interest, however, is that on the immediate right of this personification of glory that replaces and yet is so strongly reminiscent of Laura, there stand two men who seem to be escorting her at the head of the Triumph. They are Scipio and Caesar.

In an earlier version of this Triumph, apparently written during a period of enthusiasm for Caesar, Caesar was the only hero beside the goddess. In the final version, not only does Scipio stand with Caesar so near the goddess that the poet cannot perceive who stands closest (l. 24), but he is portrayed as morally superior to the great dictator. While Scipio had been a slave only of glory, Caesar had been a slave of both glory and love (ll. 22–25). The fact that the Scipio progeny far outnumbers that of the Caesars at the head of the procession leads one to feel a distinct predominance of the Scipios as devotees of glory. When we further consider that in this Triumph Petrarch marshals a huge number of past greats truly worthy of glory, whether Roman, non-Roman, or biblical heroes, Scipio occupies a conspicuous place indeed. This receives even greater emphasis from the fact that following the Scipios and the Caesars we see

Claudius Nero and Quintus Fabius Maximus, both selected for their action against the Carthaginians (ll. 45–51). And it is Hannibal himself who leads the non-Romans just ahead of Achilles, Hector and Aeneas (ll. 8–10).

All this takes us back to the "Triumph of Eternity" where we can now logically assume that among the first of "those most worthy of true Glory" (l. 127) who follow behind Laura in this triumph beyond time and death, this triumph which "God willing, we shall see up above" (ll. 122–23), are Scipio and his descendants. It also takes us back to the end of the *Africa* where Scipio's triumph established Rome once and for all as the center of the universe, and the laurel crown as a symbol of the loftiest human achievements, whether intellectual or active. When we further recall that in book 7 of the *Africa* Jove himself reveals that Rome will be "my first and greatest abode and empress of the world in eternity" (ll. 718–19), while in the *Triumphs* Scipio and Laura walk together, in the triumphs of Chastity, Glory and Eternity, we cannot help sensing a relationship between Scipio and Laura which invites comparison with the one between Beatrice and Virgil in the *Divine Comedy*. But whereas Dante had succeeded in endowing his Beatrice with those qualities that in the Christian scheme made her unquestionably superior to Virgil, Petrarch never quite succeeded in clearly distinguishing between his two paragons of human perfection. While each represents a primary aspect of earthly perfection, neither can stand alone. The great man of virtue cannot escape glory, nor can true glory be enjoyed without virtue. As the two basic components of Man's inherent greatness, they reflect the ultimate state of happiness that awaits mankind in the realm of eternity. It is interesting to note that when, at the end of the *Secretum,* St. Augustine tries to convince Petrarch that the thing to do is to "honor virtue; overlook glory and be certain that you will achieve it anyhow," Petrarch cannot accept this advice if it means abandoning his studies and his works in progress.

If we now attempt a fuller definition of the two figures, we must first note that in the "Triumph of Glory" Laura herself does not appear. While the "goddess" of the Triumph does bear a striking resemblance to Laura, as we have seen, she remains a mere symbol of glory itself. Laura reappears only in the very last Triumph, as a spirit leading those who, "in the greener and more flowering ages" of eternity (l. 133), will receive not only eternal fame but also eternal beauty. When we recall, furthermore, that in the *Secretum,* in Canzone 264 and in *Familiares* (2.9) there is also a clear distinction made between love of Laura, the lovely Lady, and love of glory, and that in both Canzone 119 and the third eclogue Laura assumes the guise of Glory only to crown a special poet on the Capitoline, a poet who had sung of a hero whose exploits are worthy not only of "sacred song" but of Orpheus (ecl. 1), we see Laura emerge as that inspiration that is at the heart of all true poetry. She is, in short, the inspiration that moves poets and men of letters to literary expression, an image of beauty and truth. It was for this reason that Petrarch was able to retain Laura as a beautiful, vibrant woman whose spirit remained with him on this earth even after death. She is as a Christian Daphne to a Christian Apollo.

Scipio, on the other hand, is the very stuff of "true" poetry: the perfect hero of Roman history, valorous and human, realistic and pious, simple and wise, caring only for things that are *optima et pulcerrima*, truly the prototype of ancient virtues. What greater exemplum could be used as incitement to moral perfection, the ultimate goal of poetry for Petrarch? Not only did he represent the triumph of Latin civilization over Carthaginian barbarism but as an individual he possessed qualities that approached perfection. Some of these we have seen already, others we shall see later. Here we shall simply elaborate on the one quality that bridges the distinction between him and Laura.

In a chapter (11) interpolated *de novo* in the last of the three redactions of the "Life of Scipio," a chapter called by De Nolhac "un morceau . . . des plus personnels, et par conséquent un des plus intéressants pour nous, de son oeuvre historique," we find a moral portrait of Scipio. Among the qualities described is Scipio's love of a particular kind of glory. Scipio himself, upon being made consul, had stated in his oration against Fabius Maximus, that throughout his life he had been possessed of an aspiration for the loftiest degree of virtue and glory. He admitted being driven by a desire "not only to equal but to surpass the distinctions of illustrious men; adding that most lofty thought, that the desire for glory extends beyond a lifetime and considers not so much the people of the present age as the memory and opinion of posterity." This is why, adds Petrarch, "it is a natural instinct of great and excellent minds to compare themselves not only to contemporaries but to men of all centuries, and to vie for fame with all." At this point Petrarch interjects a most significant remark. "This was the reason why he [Scipio] esteemed and delighted in the poets of his age; something recalled by Claudian in these verses: 'Scipio the elder, who alone turned the Punic Wars from Italian shores to their place of origin, exercised the art of arms together with that of the Muses; always did the leader display a particular care for poets.' " Petrarch then recalls how Scipio had Ennius participate in his triumph and had an image of the poet sculpted on the tomb of the Scipios. He concludes by quoting again from Claudian: "Only he who accomplishes actions worthy of poetry enjoys the virtue of having the Muses as witnesses, and loves poetry."

These verses indicate the link between Laura as poetic inspiration and Scipio as the very stuff of poetry, and in a sense, a resolution of Petrarch's conflict with respect to his love of Laura exclusively. In the third sonnet of the *Canzoniere* he ascribes the beginning of all his troubles to a Good Friday when he had first set eyes on Laura. In his "Letter to Posterity" he proudly announces that his inspiration to write the *Africa* had also come to him on a Good Friday. Similarly, the entire end of the *Secretum* seems to be a resolution of what St. Augustine considers Petrarch's two greatest faults, his love of Laura and his love of glory, in terms of his current involvement in works celebrating the great Scipio. After conceding that St. Augustine's arguments against his carnal love of Laura caused him "shame, grief, and repentance," he has the saint make two rather unexpected statements. In advising Petrarch of the many things he could turn to in order to overcome his lustful love of Laura, he reminds him "of all those works of yours that still remain unfinished and to which it would be so much more proper for you to turn instead of dividing this brief period of your existence into such unequal portions." Later, in the midst of the discussion on Petrarch's love of glory, the saint makes the previously cited statement about glory being perfectly justifiable in his eyes provided it were the natural consequence of virtue. As the discussion ends, the saint reminds Petrarch that this is the very advice that he had had Scipio's father give him in book 2 of the *Africa* (l. 486), advice that had subsequently been diligently followed by Scipio throughout his life.

If we now recall that early in his defense of his love of Laura two of Petrarch's arguments had been that "I would never have achieved this degree of renown and glory, what little it may be, if she, with the noblest sentiments, had not cultivated that most tenuous seed of virtue that nature had implanted in this breast," and, somewhat later, that "love of her, I assure you, helped me in my love of God," we see once again an implicit relationship between Laura, glory, virtue, Scipio, and the Christian ethic.

When, therefore, in the same third book of the *Secretum* we find Petrarch expressing his conviction that "that glory which is rightfully hoped for in this life ought to be sought while still here," and at the very end of the book he persists in reaching a compromise with the saint by resolving first to finish his "illustrious and outstanding" work on Scipio and then to turn to "the straight path of salvation," we sense a desperate attempt to make of Scipio what he had tried to make of Laura: a human ideal compatible with the Christian faith. There is even evidence that prior to the *Africa* Petrarch had undertaken an Italian epic to honor his favorite hero in the same language he had been using for his Laura.

ROBERT M. DURLING

The Ascent of Mt. Ventoux
and the Crisis of Allegory

My title is somewhat grandiose, I fear, and it is perhaps also somewhat ambiguous: to which crisis of allegory does it refer, to Petrarch's or to our own? These crises may be very hard to separate; they are after all historically connected, and it is difficult to avoid projecting our own critical concerns into the texts of the past. I believe it is possible to demonstrate, however, that Petrarch's letter relating his ascent of Mt. Ventoux, *Familiares* 4.1, is based on a precise and clear analysis of a problematic inherent in allegorical discourse and to some extent in discourse in general.

I shall use the term *allegory* to refer primarily to the figural relation between events: one event "means" another event, either by anticipating it, foreshadowing it, or by recalling it, fulfilling it, and thereby illuminating it. This relation involves the emergence of a paradigm or principle of relation that sets up an equivalence of some kind—usually based on analogy— between the events. It usually involved two audiences: the earlier audience and the present audience, or, in Pauline terms, those who read in the spirit and those who read in the letter (ultimately that means good readers and bad readers). To read in the letter would be to deny the relation between the Old and New Testaments as St. Paul sees it; to read in the spirit is to assert it; but to assert the figural relation between Old and New Law means adopting the New Law as the definitive interpretation of one's own experience. Hence to assert the figural relation between Old and New Testaments is to assert a relation between those books and the self and between two phases of the self (the old and the new man). A preliminary

From *Italian Quarterly* 18, no. 69 (Summer 1974). © 1974 by the University of Massachusetts.

formulation of what Petrarch is developing in his account of the ascent of Ventoux would be as follows: for experience to be valid, it must conform to the preestablished patterns provided by the religious tradition: the traditional analysis, the transition from old to new (conversion), and the examples of successful embodiment of the paradigms. But if one's experience does conform, it is suspect: it is subject to the suspicion of having been prearranged.

The letter itself falls into four parts: the preparations for the ascent; the ascent itself; the events at the summit; the descent. Each of these parts involves a critique of allegorical discourse; the critique is not always presented directly but rather emerges from the relation among the parts. In the first part, Petrarch relates that having lived all his life in view of Mt. Ventoux, he had long wished to climb it; that his desire had recently [*pridie*] been excited by his reading in Livy of Philip V of Macedon's ascent of Mt. Haemus in Thrace, from which he hoped to see both the Hellespont and the Aegean; that after mentally cataloguing and assessing his friends as possible companions he chose his brother, who was delighted to go. Several questions are implied or set afoot in this first section—the relation to a classical example; the *hantise* of a possibility long contemplated. They are to be explained more fully later. The humorously developed critique of his various friends already implies and prepares for the idea of the ascent as a figure (by synechdoche) of human life; the choice of his brother will be extremely important to the issues raised in the climb.

The second part of the letter is the ascent itself. Here the problematic begins to emerge explicitly: Is the climb allegorical? Is it possible for it not to be allegorical? If it is allegorical, what is the relation between the *real* climb and its allegorical significance? At first the ascent is easy, and during this phase they meet an aged peasant who relates that fifty years before he had made the ascent and got nothing but regret and fatigue from it; he says that no one has climbed it since then and urges them not to do so. But, says Petrarch, the young are always incredulous of those who warn them, so they go on. Now the ascent becomes more difficult; and while Gherardo, Petrarch's brother, takes the straight way up along the ridges, Petrarch seeks a more gradual path, replying to his brother's exhortations that he hopes to find an easier way on the other side. The result, related with considerable humor, is that he has to work much harder in the long run. After this has happened three or four times, he sits down in a valley and turns, he says, from the corporeal to the incorporeal, addressing to himself his allegorical reflections. The term *transiliens, leaping across,* from corporeal to incorporeal, already suggests there is a gap between them:

What you have so many times experienced in climbing this mountain, know that it happens to you and to many others as they go toward happiness (*ad beatam vitam*): but it is not considered by men so easily, since the motions of the body are visible (*in aperto*), those of the mind invisible and hidden. For what we call happiness is located on a height (*celso loco*); a narrow way, as they say, leads to it. Many hills rise up in between, and one must walk from virtue to virtue with glorious steps (*preclaris gradibus*); at the top is the goal of all and the end toward which our pilgrimage is directed. . . . What holds you back? Nothing other than the fact that the path through low earthly pleasures seems more level and, as it first appears, easier; but truly, after you have wandered a long time it will still be necessary for you to climb up to the summit of happiness though burdened with the weight of ill-delayed effort, or else to recline lazily in the valleys of your sins; and if—what I shudder to imagine—the shadow of death should find you there, to pass an eternal night in eternal sufferings. It is incredible how much this reflection aroused (*erexerit*) both body and mind to what remained [of the ascent].

(*Familiares*)

It is in no sense to minimize the moral issue to point out that the problem that underlies this passage is the relation between the real ascent and the allegorical one. It is, for one thing, supposedly discovered and asserted retrospectively, and, of course, since it is so traditional it seems facile. But the identification of the two ascents is only apparently facile; rather it is endangered by two forms of implicit critique. The physical ascent is no doubt, by synechdoche, an instance of Petrarch's characteristic mode of conduct; that is at least what he asserts, with considerable humor at his own expense. But he also maintains a disjunction between the two ascents; he calls the ascent of the real mountain *corporeal,* the ascent to virtue, *incorporeal.* What this means is that the relation between them is not reversible. Petrarch's postponing the real difficulties of the climb may be a legitimate instance of a moral flaw, but the converse is not the case: reaching the top of Ventoux may not be taken to signify an advance in virtue. "Oh, if I could only do on the spiritual level what today I have done on the bodily level," he says.

One phase of the critique of allegory, then, disjoins the concrete event (which is merely specific, relative) from the universal paradigm; it shows that climbing Ventoux is "only" corporeal. The other phase of the critique involves the same distinction and inverts means and ends. For the allegorical reflections take place at a particular point in the climb, and they have a function in the *real* climb—they give him the push he needs to reach the top. In other words, the practical significance of the spiritual reflections (and this is the whole apparatus of religious allegory, including heaven, hell, and the fear of death) is that it helps the bodily climb. This means both that the real mountain has been leveled in relation to the allegorical one (the *real* ascent does not have spiritual significance; he has NOT reached virtue), and that the allegorical mountain has been leveled by serving the real ascent.

The third section of the letter concerns the events at the summit. Here there takes place an extremely important maneuver. The allegory read into the ascent is now further discredited by being replaced by a different kind of allegory. Ascent-as-moral-progress is replaced by mountaintop-as-vantage-point. This substitution is fundamental to the strategy of the letter; it can be seen as a substitution, for the mountain as moral imperative, of Philip of Macedon's Mt. Haemus, a vantage point from which two oceans could (perhaps) be seen. For the mountain as vantage point means that the surrounding territory is *spread out* below, evened out for the view. The significance of the first part of the letter will be revealed partly in terms of the tension between these two possible kinds of allegory.

After admiring the impression of height, the clouds being below his feet, Petrarch turns east toward the Alps, and yearns toward Italy. He remembers how Hannibal crossed the Alps, and then a new thought, he says, drew his reflections over [*traduxit*] from space to time. For the second time in the letter he addresses himself:

> Today the tenth year is completed since you left Bologna and your boyhood studies.... How many changes the time in between has seen! I am not yet in port ... perhaps the time will come when I can say with Augustine, "I wish to remember my past filthiness." ... But much still remains to me of round-about (*ambigui*) and painful work.... What I used to love I no longer love. I lie: I love, but more sparingly. Behold, I have lied again: I love, but more shamefastly, more sadly. At last I have spoken the truth: so it is, I love, but what I would rather not love, what I wish to hate; I love, but unwilling, coerced.... Not yet has the third year passed by from which that perverse will that had me totally and reigned without contradiction in

the palace of my heart began to have another one rebelling and
fighting against it.

So in his thought, he says, he turned over the decade, revolved
through it. Then he turns to the future:

> If you live for another ten years and move toward virtue as
> much as you have in these last ten years, perhaps at forty you
> will have reached a point from which you can readily go on to
> the next life [I paraphrase here].

What this passage emphasizes is the connection between the vantage
point of the mountaintop as a place of detached contemplation and the
emergence to explicitness of the difficulty of speaking the truth. He has
gone over from space (the land evened out below) to time (time evened out
below), and this vantage is clearly related to the image he uses in *Familiares*
1.1, which dedicates the entire collection to Socrates. He has been going
through old papers and letters, he says, and he is sitting surrounded by
confused heaps of paper—as it were, by the lesser peaks of a mountain
range. His impulse is to burn them all. But he addresses to himself the
following reflections:

> What prohibits you, I say, like a traveler wearied by his long
> journey, from looking back as from a height (*e specula*) and
> step by step measuring the cares of your youth?

The detachment implied in both these metaphors is only relative, of
course. He is still *in via*. But still there is an eminence; he gets out of
involvement, looks backward and forward calmly.

As he looks backward, he attempts to define his situation, in particular the state of his will. He might be tempted, by the fact that he has
reached some kind of height, to suppose that he has reached virtue. But he
can see clearly what is wrong with his claims, and he winnows a series of
"lies" until he reaches what he regards as an accurate statement. There
are two principles at work here, and in Petrarch they seem to be inescapably connected. There is the insistence on sharp criticism of claims to moral
progress, a retrospect on successive formulations that probes each for its
possible falsity. The critique is possible because of the detachment, so
different from the impulse to complete the climb that resulted from his
earlier words to himself. The critique of the lie, then, brings to explicitness
the earlier disjunction of the real from the allegorical goal. But it is partly
the detachment, partly the satisfaction inherent in seeing clearly, in

winnowing the lies, that leads to the second principle, a certain disarming of the existential urgency. Petrarch's situation in his struggle is midway— ten years from its beginning, ten years from its imagined conclusion. The struggle between the two wills is going on as well as we have any right to expect.

As Professors Courcelle, Rico, and Billanovich have pointed out, there are many parallels in the passage we have just been looking at with book 8 of Augustine's *Confessions,* with the *Secretum,* with Ovid, and with Seneca. This literary elaborateness serves a definite function. The fact that the very passage which criticizes the successive lies is derived from Seneca in itself raises the very question of authenticity that Petrarch is focusing on. Of course my point is that it is meant to; I shall return to this idea later.

Now Petrarch turns west and describes the view of France, thus returning from *time* to *space,* and, appropriately enough for someone whose moral struggle is going well enough, his thoughts float suspended, now savoring of heaven, now of earth. At the moment of his relative satisfaction with himself, then, comes the famous incident of the oracle. Here I must quote more extensively, and I shall continue into the fourth part, for, as you will notice, Petrarch's reflections on the oracle are represented as taking place during the descent.

> As I look at all these things and now savor a bit of earth, now after the example of my body lifts my spirit to higher things, I decided (*visum est michi*) to look into Augustine's *Confessions,* your kind gift, which to remind me of the giver I have always with me and in my hands, a book that fits your hand, small in volume but of infinite sweetness. I open it, to read whatever I found: what indeed could I find except something pious and devout? By chance (*forte*) the tenth book of the work presented itself. My brother, expecting to hear something of Augustine's through my mouth, was all ears. I call God to witness and my brother, who was there: where I first set down my eyes was written, "And men go about to admire high mountains and the great floods of the sea and the broad streams of the rivers and the surrounding ocean, and the circles of the stars; and themselves they leave behind." I was amazed, I say. And, asking my brother, who was anxious to hear, not to bother me, I closed the book, angry with myself that even now I should still be looking at earthly things, who ought long ago to have learned from the very pagan philosophers that there is nothing worthy

of admiration except the mind (*animum*), since to a great spirit nothing is great.

Then indeed, satisfied to have seen enough of the mountain, I turned my inner eyes on myself; and from that hour, no one heard me say anything until we reached the bottom: those words gave me enough to do in silence. Nor could I believe that it had happened fortuitously; but I considered that whatever I had read there was said for me and no one else, remembering that once Augustine suspected the same thing about himself when in reading the volume of the Apostle the first thing that met him was this: "Not in banquets and drunkenness, not in chambering and wantonness, not in contention and emulation, but put on the Lord Jesus Christ and make no provision for the flesh of your lusts." Which had previously happened to Anthony, when, hearing the Gospel where it is written, "If you would be perfect, go and sell all that you have and give to the poor and come and follow me, and you will have a treasure in Heaven," as if this scripture had been recited for him, as his biographer Athanasius says, he took on the obedience of the Lord. And just as Anthony, having heard this, asked no further; and as Augustine, having read this, went no further; so for me the end of the whole reading was the words I have cited above; and in silence I considered how great is the futility of human counsels that, neglecting the noblest part of themselves, they diffuse themselves in vain spectacles, seeking without what they could find within; and I admired the nobility of our mind, if only it had not gone astray from its noble origins and had not turned into shame what God gave it for an honor. How many times, do you think, though I kept on walking, did I turn back and look at the summit of the mountain! and it seemed barely a cubit high in comparison with the heights the mind can reach contemplation when one has not immersed it in the mud of earthly filth.

Now the moment of the oracle is characteristically Petrarchan; it is of a kind that boggles readers, like the revelation that it is the tenth anniversary of his leaving Bologna, or the arrival on the same day of the coronation invitations from Paris and Rome (*Fam.* 4.4). Surely, readers say, if these assertions are true, they were planned into the events. How can the oracle be taken seriously? they say; The spine of his book must have been cracked, or he had a bookmark in book 10. The question of Petrarch's seriousness tends to be identified with that of his veracity. Professor [Pierre] Courcelle writes:

> Is it a mere pastiche, then? It is certain that at the moment of writing Petrarch knows very well the literary antecedents of his letter: not only the *Confessions,* but also another scene of "sortes biblicae" referred to by Augustine, St. Anthony taking as a personal admonition the verse that he hears being read in church. Petrarch even took pains to look up the life of Anthony by Athanasius, and he cites it in Evagrius' translation. He skillfully introduces the passage from the *Confessions* by describing the mountains, the coast, the course of the Rhone as they appear from Ventoux. Above all, one phrase of Petrarch's must provoke a certain malaise, this oath: "I call upon God to witness." [. . .] One is right therefore to ask if Petrarch gives us the facts like a historian, with perfect veracity. But it seems to me hasty to conclude, like von Martin, that it is a mere charade.
>
> *(Les Confessions de saint Augustin dans la tradition littéraire. Antécédents et postérite)*

But what is a "charade"? May that not on occasion be a very serious matter? To take the points mentioned by Professor Courcelle in order: the presence of Augustine's and Anthony's *sortes* in the passage *raises the question* of the relation of Petrarch's experience to those precedents. The description of the landscape is part of the appositeness of the oracle, which mentions precisely the items Petrarch says he has been looking at. The oath *calls attention* to the possibility that this is fiction (just as the meditation on the descent considers whether it is chance). The question of the seriousness of the letter is put there by Petrarch himself; *he* is raising these questions that haunt his interpreters—the seriousness lies precisely in the necessity of questioning the event.

At this point it is necessary to consider the relation of Petrarch's oracle to Augustine's (and, incidentally, to Anthony's), for the difference between them is, I think, the key to the structure of the letter. Petrarch's mountaintop is very different from Augustine's garden. In book 7 of the *Confessions* we have witnessed Augustine's acceptance of the concept of spirit and of the intellectual truth of Christian faith. In book 8 the issue is a practical one—what kind of life to follow? more important, how to resolve the split in his own will that holds back his commitment to Christian abstinence and to a monastic way of life. The crisis in the garden is represented as revolving precisely around his relation to *examples*. Early in book 8, Augustine hears from Simplicianus the story of Victorinus, and he "burns" to imitate him. When he hears from Ponticianus the stories of Anthony and the converts of Trèves, the example makes him realize his own deformity, and the pain of this knowledge, of the contrast between his inactivity and entanglement in pleasure and their decisiveness is what precipitates the storm of tears in the garden and leads to the consultation of the oracle. Let me list the elements in these stories that are related to the scene in the garden.

A. 1. Anthony is trying to decide what to do with his wealth.
   2. He enters Church.
   3. He hears a verse from the Gospel being read aloud.
   4. He immediately applies it to himself and follows it.
   5. He later receives a second oracle in the same way (it is the same verse), about what provision to make for his sister.

B. 1. The *agentes in rebus* walk in a garden, at random.
   2. They happen upon a monastery and enter it.
   3. They find a book of the life of Anthony there; one of them reads it.
   4. The one reading is fired to imitate the saint, and he expresses his desire to his companion.
   5. Together they decide on the spot to imitate the saint by joining the monastery that very day. (Later, their fiancées follow their example.)

Now there is not a single item here that is not included, sometimes in very changed form, of course, in the scene in the garden. My point, however, is not that Augustine's account is derivative, but rather how he represents the function of the precedents. For Augustine, at least as he represents it here, the scene in the garden was a turning point because he discovered how to resynthesize the elements into an experience combining precedent and originality.

On the day of the scene in the garden, all the force of these examples is brought to bear on Augustine, and it is clear he thought of that as providential. And it cannot be emphasized too strongly that, although he has known Ponticianus for some time, this is the *first time* he has heard from him, the first time he has been confronted with the examples of Anthony and the *Agentes*.

C. 1. Ponticianus happens to come to Augustine's house, for some indifferent purpose (cf. A.1, B.1, 2).

2. He happens to find (*forte attendit*) a book on the gaming table; he takes it up and opens it (B.3).

3. He is surprised to find it is the epistles of Paul, and he narrates the stories of Anthony and the *Agentes*.

4. As he listens to Ponticianus, Augustine confronts his own state and retrospectively reflects on the twelve years since he read Cicero's *Hortensius* (B.4).

5. After the departure of Ponticianus, Augustine goes outside into the garden, as far as possible from the house, in a fever to imitate the *Agentes* (B.1, 4). He expresses this to Alypius (B.5).

6. His conflict is formulated and analyzed as an instance of conflict of flesh and spirit in Romans 7.

7. He goes as far as possible from Alypius, throws himself down under the fig tree, and weeps, crying "How long? how long tomorrow and tomorrow? why not now? why not this very hour an end to my deformity?"

8. He hears the voice crying "Tolle, lege" (A.2).

9. He decides that he is being divinely instructed to seek an oracle in the Epistles, as Anthony had by hearing the Gospel (B.4).

10. He returns to Alypius, where he had left the book, opens it, and reads Romans 13:13 (B.3).

11. He accepts the oracle; his split is healed (A.4).

12. He relates this to Alypius, keeping his finger in the book (B.4).

13. Alypius requests an oracle and receives Romans 14:1, the succeeding verse (A.5).

14. Alypius accepts the oracle and joins Augustine (B.5).

15. Together they reenter the house and announce the events to Augustine's mother (B.6).

In other words, Augustine succeeds in combining elements from all the examples in a way that is uniquely his own. The incident has indoor and outdoor phases, like that of both Anthony and the *Agentes*. Like the *Agentes*, Augustine imitates Anthony; but he does so in a way that surpasses theirs in closeness to the model, since it includes an oracle. Like Anthony's, his instruction has two phases; but unlike the illiterate Anthony, Augustine both *hears* and *reads*. Like the *Agentes*, he gives an immediate account of himself (again, twice). Like the first *Agens* he brings along his companion (as Anthony had brought along his sister). That the oracle itself is the crossing point for Augustine expresses the necessity of a certain crystallization of the reading of St. Paul; and it is led up to by the realization of the validity of the theoretical paradigm, St. Paul's analysis in Romans 7. When Augustine accepts Romans 13:13 as *applying directly to him,* he eliminates the gap he has been experiencing between word and event: he accepts identity with the referent of the text, and so the split within himself is healed. He begins immediately reading himself in the spirit instead of in the letter. The models are imitated and the patterns fulfilled in an authentic new event; the individual is possessed by his significance.

Like Augustine's *sortes,* Petrarch's experience of the oracle is the climax of a process of tropological identifications, but, as we have already seen, one of a rather different nature. As a matter of fact the parallels between the texts are extensive, and I hope I may be forgiven if I continue the rather mechanical procedure of listing.

ASCENT.
1. Petrarch is on an excursion with a companion (the mountain thus corresponds to both the garden in Milan and the one in Trèves).
2. Petrarch is outstripped by his companion (cf. A.5, B.5, C.7 and 14).
3. Part way up the slope, Petrarch reflects on his difficulties (cf. C.5, halfway in the account between the house and the fig tree).
4. Petrarch goes as far up the mountain as he can (cf. C.7), rejoining his companion (Augustine is separating himself from his companion).

SUMMIT (Petrarch is now at the point that corresponds to the fig tree).
5. Petrarch meditates on the ten years since he left Bologna (C.4).
6. The battle between two wills began three years ago (cf. C.6, where the battle between the two wills is at its high point *now*).
7. In perhaps ten more years he will have been victorious (cf. C.7: "How long tomorrow and tomorrow?").
8. Turning west, Petrarch decides to open the *Confessions* (cf. C.9–10: Augustine has heard the voice and has returned to Alypius).

9. Petrarch reads *Confessions* 10.8.5 (C.10).
10. Petrarch does accept the oracle, but he does not read aloud; instead, he asks his brother not to disturb him (C.11–12, B.4). (And so Gherardo not only does not get an oracle of his own, he does not even hear Francesco's.)

DESCENT.

11. Petrarch decides the oracle is not fortuitous, citing the precedents of Augustine and Anthony (C.3, 9).

Now the striking thing about this series is that almost without exception the parallels are negative. In place of the integrative, resynthesizing process of Augustine's experience, we find disjunction, the dissolution of possible connections, negative parallels. The changes in order of some of the elements, furthermore, as we have already seen, deprive the oracle on Ventoux of any of the existential urgency it possessed for Augustine; the top of the mountain has been reached; the allegorical meaning of ascent has been both explained and discredited; the long-term struggle with fleshliness has also been dealt with. No decision is reached by Petrarch, no change of profession. There is only an act of reading, and even that remains silent. Petrarch's oracle, then, restates and contains all the earlier instances of negative relation to models; it is the negative fulfillment of the entire letter.

From the vantage of Mt. Ventoux, we see that the garden, for the converts of Trèves and for Augustine, is indeed a place of collection, but it is not an image of detachment, rather it is a deep internal space, the deepest possible involvement in one's situation, the most intense mustering of resources. There, as into a womb, the fructifying Word penetrates and the self is reborn. For Augustine the garden is obviously related figurally to Eden; it is a place of fruitfulness, of the experience of presence. For Petrarch the mountaintop is an experience of absence. And Petrarch's oracle involves a reformulation of the perspective that calls into question the entire climb, including the earlier allegoresis. When Augustine is invoked, the implication would seem to be that Petrarch should stay at home and climb the *true* allegorical mountains, rather than speculate on the gaps between them and *real* mountains. This is, of course, the reason for his anger. At a moment when he was not expecting it, the text has somehow encircled him and contained him; undermining the very struggle for authenticity we examined above. Thus we have a combination of disjunction and return that is strikingly similar to the Freudian analysis of the mechanisms of paranoia. In any case, the experience of encirclement and the calling into question of all facile allegories, is characteristic of *irony*, and I would like to suggest that irony is the negative form of allegory. If allegory joins two events in a proposition that sees fulfillment, irony disjoins two events by denying or frustrating fulfillment. If allegorical reading of the self accepts identity with examples, ironic reading of the self measures the distance from them, and disjoins two moments or aspects of the self in a critique of the inauthenticity that had seemed to join them.

Of course the most immediate model whose example Petrarch is not following in the ascent is his brother Gherardo, and the difference between their paths has long been taken to refer to Gherardo's conversion to Carthusian monasticism in 1343, and thus as evidence that the letter could not have been written at its ostensible date, 1336. Recently Giles Constable observed that there is no mention of Gherardo on the descent, as if he had stayed on the mountaintop. And the exclusion of Gherardo from the experience of the oracle, the emphasis that the words were addressed to Petrarch alone, is part of a pattern that exempts Gherardo from the difficulties, both allegorical and ironic, of the excursion. Gherardo is distinguished from Francesco within the letter almost as an *Ansich* from a *Fürscich*. He is not tormented by the problems of consciousness and self-consciousness that permeate the letter. One thing that is strongly suggested by the letter is that, whatever the appropriate interpretation of Gherardo's experience may be, Petrarch himself must be on guard against facile moralistic claims about himself. If the letter does refer to Gherardo's monastic conversion, then, it must be seen also as a defense against the supposition that coming down again—not joining a monastery—is somehow "not serious."

Petrarch's reflections on the way down the mountain provide one of the most troubling issues which his critical awareness sees. For as he comes down the mountain, considering whether the oracle could have been fortuitous, his thoughts remount time (just as he frequently looks back up toward the summit). What is revealed as the precedents are listed in a progressive de-intensification, a de-gradation that is inherent in the history of Christianity, or at least in the problematic of imitation as Petrarch sees it. The more often basic patterns are imitated, the more diluted the imitations become.

> Anthony's oracle was the Gospel.
> Augustine's oracle was the Apostle.
> Petrarch's is a patristic writer.

Anthony *heard* the text being read aloud.
Augustine was directed by a voice to *read*.
Petrarch, by chance or habit, *read*.

Anthony sold his possessions and became an anchorite.
Augustine was baptised and took up a monastic life.
Petrarch—turned his inward eyes on himself.

It is particularly noteworthy that it is the newness of Anthony's example that moves Augustine; he has a sense of the historical urgency of the emergent monastic movement. He responds immediately. But Petrarch comes nine hundred years later. The example of Anthony and Augustine, not to speak of Christ and the Apostles, are not something he has only learned about today—they are the models he has been confronted with since childhood, like Mt. Ventoux itself. The newness of example that moves Petrarch, according to his account, is the reading, *pridie,* of the example of Philip of Macedon's climbing of Mt. Haemus, whose importance in the letter we are perhaps now in a better position to appreciate. If at the top of Mt. Ventoux we move from space to time, it is not only in terms of the last ten years and the next ten years. For the first thing that the Alps suggest to Petrarch in the way of time, is the memory of Hannibal. The mountain-as-vantage-point is an image of the historical situation of a critical consciousness that has an entirely new fullness of knowledge and perspective on the two worlds—ancient and medieval—represented by Rome and Paris or Italy and France. From this eminence the differences between pagan thought and Christian thought seem to be relatively evened out. The pagan philosophers teach the same lessons as Augustine, at least insofar as they are reduced to the single antithesis of the opposition between flesh and spirit.

JOHN FRECCERO

The Fig Tree and the Laurel:
Petrarch's Poetics

After six centuries Petrarch's reputation as the first humanist remains unshaken. Cultural historians have generally accepted his own estimate of himself as the man who inaugurated a new era, leaving behind him what he called "the dark ages." His reputation as a poet is equally secure, at least in the literary histories; he is in many respects the most influential poet in the history of Western literature. Critics have failed, however, to define adequately the ways in which his poetry was as revolutionary as his humanistic writings. The poetics of the *Canzoniere* remain as elusive as the persona that emerges from its lyrics. The purpose of this essay is to offer a tentative definition and to suggest the ways in which Petrarch's greatest work deserves its reputation as the precursor of modern poetry.

Petrarch's poetic achievement, for all its grandeur, would appear to be decidedly conservative with respect to the Middle Ages. Far from repudiating the verse forms of his predecessors, he brought them to technical perfection and established them as models for future generations of poets. The poems of the *Canzoniere* seem to be crystallizations of previously invented verse forms: the sonnet, the sestina, the Dantesque canzone. In content, they are equally familiar, not to say banal, for they elaborate with spectacular variations a tired theme of courtly love: the idolatrous and unrequited passion for a beautiful and sometimes cruel lady. Apart from the extensive use of classical myth, there is little that is radically new in the thematics of the *Canzoniere*.

The extraordinary innovation in the *Canzoniere* is rather to be found

From *Literary Theory/Renaissance Texts*, edited by Patricia Parker and David Quint. © 1986 by the Johns Hopkins University Press, Baltimore/London.

in what the verses leave unsaid, in the blank spaces separating these lyric "fragments," as they were called, from each other. The persona created by the serial juxtaposition of dimensionless lyric moments is as illusory as the animation of a film strip, the product of the reader's imagination as much as of the poet's craft; yet, the resultant portrait of an eternally weeping lover remains Petrarch's most distinctive poetic achievement. Because it is a composite of lyric instants, the portrait has no temporality; only the most naive reader would take it for authentic autobiography. For the same reason, it is immune from the ravages of time, a mood given a fictive *durée* by the temporality of the reader, or a score to be performed by generations of readers from the Renaissance to the Romantics. It remained for centuries the model of poetic self-creation even for poets who, in matters of form, thought of themselves as anti-Petrarchan.

Literary self-creation in the Middle Ages could not fail to evoke the name of Saint Augustine, the founder of the genre. The *Confessions,* Petrarch's favorite book, is at the same time the model for much of Petrarch's description of the lover as sinner. Both stories are ostensibly attempts to recapture a former self in a retrospective literary structure, a narrative of conversion (*Canzoniere* 1.4: "quand' era in parte altr'uom da quel ch'i'sono"), but Petrarch makes no claim to reality or to moral witness. Instead, he uses Augustinian principles in order to create a totally autonomous portrait of the artist, devoid of any ontological claim. The moral struggle and the spiritual torment described in the *Canzoniere* are, as we shall see, part of a poetic strategy. When the spiritual struggle is demystified, its poetic mechanism is revealed: the petrified idolatrous lover is an immutable monument to Petrarch, his creator and namesake. In this sense, the laurel, the emblem both of the lover's enthrallment and of the poet's triumph, is the antitype of Augustine's fig tree, under which the saint's conversion took place. The fig tree was already a scriptural emblem of conversion before Augustine used the image in his *Confessions* to represent the manifestation of the pattern of universal history in his own life. Petrarch's laurel, on the other hand, has no such moral dimension of meaning. It stands for a poetry whose real subject matter is its own act and whose creation is its own author.

The two emblems, the fig tree and the laurel, may be said to stand respectively, as we shall see, for different modes of signification: the allegorical and the autoreflexive. The first is the mode characteristic of Christian typology, while the second, extended over the course of the entire narrative, is Petrarch's own. The fig tree and the laurel stand for the two poles of a verbal universe whose principles were shared by Augustine and the poet. Before defining the differences between them more precisely, we must turn to review some of those principles.

For Augustine, consciousness begins in desire. To discover the self is to discover it as in some sense lacking, absent to itself, and desire is the soul's reaching out to fill the void. This reaching out toward an as-yet-unspecified object is at the same time the birth of language, or at least of the paralanguage of gesticulation, literally a reaching out toward signification. The first chapters of the *Confessions* represent language and desire as indistinguishable, perhaps even coextensive. The child learns to speak in order to express its desire; at the same time, however, it learns what to desire from a world of objects that adults have named. Language is not only the vehicle of desire, it is also in some sense its creator, first through the agency of others, the mother and the nurse, and ultimately, sometimes insidiously, through the power of literary suggestion. From the first words of the child to the final utterance, the process remains essentially the same: far from being the sole interpreters of the words we use, we are at the same time interpreted by them. For Augustine, then, as for contemporary semiologists, man *is* his own language, for his desires and his words are inseparable.

If this is so, it follows that the end terms of both language and desire are one and the same. So it is, inevitably, in a theology of the Word. The ultimate end of desire is God, in whom the soul finds its satisfaction. The ultimate end of signification is a principle of intelligibility in terms of which all things may be understood. God the Word is at once the end of all desire and the ultimate meaning of all discourse. In the ninth book of the *Confessions,* just before the death of Monica, Augustine speaks of language in terms of desire and of desire in terms of language:

> If, for any man, the tumult of the flesh were silent: if the images of the earth, the waters and the air were silent: if the poles were silent; if the soul itself were silent and transcended itself by not thinking about itself . . . if they were silent and He spoke . . . by Himself, Whom we love in these things; were we to hear Him without them and if it continued like this, would it not be entering into the joy of the Lord?
>
> (9.10)

All creation is a discourse leading to Love, just as all desire is ultimately a desire for the Word. The theology of the Word binds together language and desire by ordering both to God, in whom they are grounded. From a naturalistic standpoint, it is impossible to say whether human discourse is a reflection of the word or whether the idea of God is simply a metaphoric application of linguistic theory. Whether we accept Augustine's theology in some form or translate it into what might be called a semiology of desire, we remain within a verbal universe, reaching out for a silent terminal point that lies outside the system.

The Word, the silence that subtends the system, grounds both desire and language. In its absence, however, both threaten to become an infinite regression, approaching ultimate satisfaction and ultimate significance as an unreachable limit. This is probably most clear in terms of Augustinian desire, which is insatiable in human terms. Each of the successive desires of life are in fact desires for selfhood, expressed metonymically in an ascending hierarchy of abstraction: nourishment for the child, sex for the adolescent, fame for the adult. In an Augustinian world, there is no escape from desire short of God: "Our heart [he says] is unquiet until it rest in Thee" (*Confessions* 1.1).

As all desire is ultimately a desire for God, so all signs point ultimately to the Word. In a world without ultimate significance, there is no escape from the infinite referentiality of signs. Signs, like desire, continually point beyond themselves. In the *De Magistro,* for example, Augustine says that signs cannot convince an unbeliever, but can only point in the direction of reality. For the unbeliever to perceive the Truth, Christ must teach him from within. Short of the Word made flesh, there can be no bridge between words and things: "All other things may be expressed in some way; He alone is ineffable, Who spoke and all things were made. He spoke and we were made; but we are unable to speak of Him. His Word, by Whom we were spoken, is His Son. He was made weak, so that He might be spoken by us, despite our weakness."

In our own day, we have learned about the infinite referentiality of signs, "unlimited semiosis," from Saussure and from Peirce, among others. Anterior to the written text is the spoken text, anterior to that is the acoustic image, in turn dependent upon a concept that is itself linguistically structured. Our attempt to make the leap from words to things seems doomed to a continual feedback that looks like infinite regression. C. S. Peirce speaks of the phenomenon in terms that are reminiscent of the *De Magistro*:

> The object of representation can be nothing but a representation of which the first representation is the interpretant. But an endless series of representations, each representing the one behind it, may be conceived to have an absolute object at

> its limit. . . . Finally, the interpretant is nothing but another
> representation *to which the torch of truth is handed along* and
> as representation, it has its interpretant again. Lo, another
> infinite series.

For Augustine, the central metaphor of Christianity provided the grounding for this infinite regression. Reality itself is linguistically structured. It is
God's book, having him for both its author and its subject matter. Words
point to things, but those things are themselves signs pointing to God, the
ultimately signified. The metaphor of God's book halts the infinite series
by ordering all signs to itself. In germ, this is the foundation of Christian
allegory and of salvation history.

The fig tree, in Augustine's narrative, is a sign, just as it is in the
gospels when Christ says to his disciples that they must look to the fig tree
if they would read the signs of the apocalyptic time. The fig tree in the
garden of Milan, in the eighth book of the *Confessions,* for all its historicity, is at the same time meant to represent the broader pattern of salvation
history for all Christians. The moment represents the revelation of God's
Word at a particular time and place, recapitulating the Christ event in an
individual soul. Behind that fig tree stands a whole series of anterior
images pointing backward to Genesis; Augustine's reader is meant to
prolong the trajectory by applying it to his own life and extending it
proleptically toward the ending of time.

In the Old Testament, the prophet Micah looks forward to the day
when the promise will be fulfilled: "He shall sit every man under his vine
and under his fig tree" (Mic. 4:4). The hope of the Jews, their nationhood,
is represented by the same tree that in Genesis suggested their estrangement from God. At the beginning of the Gospel of John, the words of the
prophet are perhaps recalled when Nathanael is called out from under the
fig tree by the Messiah: "Before Philip called thee, when thou wast under
the fig tree, I saw thee" (John 1:48). So in the *Confessions,* Augustine's
calling, in the voices of children who sing "tolle, lege," takes place under
the tree of Micah and Nathanael, whatever its botanical species. The
paradigm of salvation history is made manifest at the end of an historical
evolution and provides another "testament" to the interpretation of a man
by God's Word.

Because Augustine's narrative is patterned after the same model that
he took to be the principle of intelligibility in all human reality, the
question of its historicity is meaningless. It might be said that the redemption itself depends upon a literary understanding of God's relationship to

the world: the manifestation, at the end of a syntagmatic chain, of a significance present from the beginning. Like the intentionality of a sentence that preexists in its utterance and emerges concretely, in retrospect, from that utterance, the uncreated Word produces its signifier and is in turn made manifest by it. Like language, the Redemption is tautology, ending where it began. Exactly the same relationship exists between Augustine's narrative and the reality it presumably represents. Is the story that we read a faithful portrayal of a life interpreted by God, or is that conversion experience the illusory feedback of plot structure in a narrative of the self? Conversion demands that there be both a continuity and a discontinuity between the self that *is* and the self that *was*. Similarly, a narrative of the self demands that author and persona be distinguished until they are fused at the narrative's culminating moment. Just as it is impossible to say whether God's presence is the reality of the Bible or the illusory projection of it, so it is impossible to say whether the conversion experience is the cause or the creature of the narrative that we read. When language in some form, however metaphorical, is the ultimate reality, we must be content with words upon words.

It must not be imagined that this is a modern distortion of Augustine's conception of his enterprise. In the text of the *Confessions*, conversion is always a literary event, a gloss on an anterior text. He correctly interprets the voices of the children to be a command to pick up the Bible and read a passage at random because he remembered Ponticianus's story of the two men who read the life of Antony and were thereupon converted. Antony himself, he remembered, "happened to go into a church while the gospel was being read and had taken it as a counsel addressed to himself when he heard the words, 'Go home and sell all that belongs to you . . . and follow me.' By this divine pronouncement he had at once been converted to You" (8.12). So Augustine picks up the Bible and reads the passage that interprets him and is thereby converted. The following moment points to his newly acquired vocation, for he then passes the Bible to his friend Alypius, thereby suggesting that his own text is to be applied proleptically to the reader himself as a part of the continual unfolding of God's Word in time. Consequently, the "truth-value" of Augustine's narrative depends, not upon its hypothetical conformity to brute "fact," supposing such a thing to exist, nor upon the illusory projection of human representation, but upon the arbitrary privilege granted to God's Word as the ultimate significance of all discourse. The fig tree, under the shade of which all this takes place, stands for a tradition of textual anteriority that extends backward in time to the Logos and forward to the same Logos at time's ending, when both desire and words are finally fulfilled: "Justi et sancti fruuntur Verbo Dei sine lectione, sine litteris."

We must turn now, for contrast, to a passage in the first book of Petrarch's *Secretum*, in which Francesco is scolded by his fictive interlocutor, Augustine, for a moral weakness with which they were both familiar: a certain paralysis of the will. Augustine reassures Francesco by describing his own conversion.

> AUGUSTINE: Yet, for all that, I remained the man I had been
>   before, when finally a profound meditation brought before
>   my eyes all of my unhappiness. Thus, from the moment
>   that I willed it fully and completely, I found the power to
>   do it, and with a marvelous and joyful rapidity, I was
>   transformed into another Augustine, whose story I believe
>   you know from my *Confessions*.
> FRANCESCO: I know it, of course: nor can I ever forget that
>   life-giving fig tree, under whose shadow this miracle hap-
>   pened to you.
> AUGUSTINE: I should hope not, for neither myrtle nor ivy, nor
>   even that laurel dear (so they say) to Phoebus, should be so
>   welcome to you. Even if the entire chorus of poets should
>   yearn for that laurel and you above all, who alone among
>   all of your contemporaries were worthy to have its sought-
>   after leaves as your crown, yet the remembrance of that
>   fig tree should be dearer, if, after many tempests, you one
>   day arrive in port, for it portends a sure hope of correc-
>   tion and pardon.

The note of preciosity, here as elsewhere in the *Secretum*, derives from the fact that since both voices are Petrarch's the inconclusive conversation about moral paralysis constitutes an elegant dramatization of its own subject matter. Like the historical Augustine whom he so much admired, Petrarch was expert at drawing real literary strength from fictionalized moral flaws. Of much more interest, however, is the very un-Augustinian homage that Augustine pays to the poet laureate, thereby betraying the real point of the exchange. Francesco compliments Augustine for the *Confessions* and acknowledges the fig tree as an example for all men. The laurel, however, the symbol of poetic supremacy, is his alone. We must turn now to the implications of Petrarch's claim.

We have seen that the fig tree is an allegorical sign. It stands for a referential series of anterior texts grounded in the Logos. It is at once unique, as the letter must be, and yet referential, pointing to a truth beyond itself, a spiritual sense. While it is true that the being of the letter cannot be doubted, its meaning transcends it in importance. As all signs point ultimately to God, so it may be said that all books, for the Augustinian, are in some sense copies of God's Book. When Dante affirms that he is simply a scribe, copying down the words that love dictates to him, he is echoing this theory. On the other hand, for the laurel to be truly unique, it cannot *mean* anything: its referentiality must be neutralized if it is to remain the property of its creator. Petrarch makes of it the emblem of the mirror relationship *Laura-Lauro,* which is to say, the poetic lady created by the poet, who in turn creates him as poet laureate. This circularity forecloses all referentiality and in its self-contained dynamism resembles the inner life of the Trinity as the Church fathers imagined it. One could scarcely suppose a greater autonomy. This poetic strategy corresponds, in the theological order, to the sin of idolatry.

In his *Religion of Israel* (trans. M. Greenberg), Yehezkel Kaufmann has shown that the Jews' conception of idolatry was a kind of fetishism, the worship of reified signs devoid of significance. The gods of the gentiles were coextensive with their representations, as though they dwelt not on Olympus or in the skies, but within a golden calf, a stone, or a piece of wood. Signs point to an absence or a significance yet to come; they are in this sense allegorical. Idols, as the Jews understood them, like fetishes, were a desperate attempt to render *presence,* a reified sign, one might almost say a metaphor. It is almost as if the gentiles, in the Jews' reading, sought to evade the temporality inherent in the human condition by reifying their signs and thereby eternalizing significance in the here and now. Stones are mute, but as a compensation they last forever.

This theological problematic has its exact counterpart in the linguistic realm, except that its terms are reversed: in order to create an autonomous universe of autoreflexive signs without reference to an anterior logos—the dream of almost every poet since Petrarch—it is necessary that the thematic of such poetry be equally autoreflexive and self-contained, which is to say, that it be idolatrous in the Augustinian sense. The idolatrous love for Laura, however self-abasing it may seem, has the effect of creating a thoroughly autonomous portrait of the poet who creates it; its circular referentiality, like that of the Trinity (Father, Son, and the Love that binds them), cannot be transcended at a higher order. The laurel lives forever, no matter what happened to Francesco. This is the human strategy, the demystification of Petrarch's deliberately idolatrous pose. If the gentiles, in the Jews' interpretation of them, sought to make their gods present by reifying their signs, then we might say that Petrarch sought to reify his signs, objectify his poetic work, by making his "god," the lady Laura, the object of his worship. Critics given to psychologizing have repeatedly tried to reconstruct Petrarch's spiritual torment from his verses; where language is the only reality, however, it would be more prudent to see the spiritual torment as the reflection, the thematic translation, of his autoreflexive poetics.

We may observe in passing that the semiological meaning of idolatry, that is, the reification of the sign in an attempt to create poetic presence, is consonant with Augustine's sign theory. In the first chapter of the *De Doctrina Christiana*, in the middle of a discussion of the referentiality of signs, he introduces his famous distinction concerning human desire (1.2): God alone is to be enjoyed [*frui*], all other things are to be used [*uti*]. Sin consists in enjoying that which should be used. The distinction seems somewhat out of place until we recall that all things are signs and that God is the terminal point on a referential chain. Once language is equated with desire, then it is clear that to deprive signs of their referentiality and to treat a poetic statement as autonomous, an end in itself, is the definition of idolatry.

Perhaps the most obvious example of Petrarch's attempt to short-circuit the referentiality of his signs is to be found in the sestina numbered 30 in the *Canzoniere:* "Giovene donna sotto un verde lauro." Augustine's conversion took place in a single moment, the *kairos,* in the shadow of the fig tree. Petrarch transforms the moment into a cyclical lifetime in the shadow of the laurel:

> seguiró l'ombra di quel dolce lauro
> per lo più ardente sole e per la neve,
> fin che l'ultimo dí chiuda quest'occhi.

[I shall follow the shadow of that sweet laurel in the most ardent sun or through the snow, until the last day closes these eyes.]

The *lauro* here represents the lady, whose shadow the lover will follow all the days of his life, just as the lover in Dante's sestina, from which Petrarch's is derived, spends all of his time searching "dove suoi panni fanno ombra." Because Petrarch's *lauro* is literally a tree, however, that symbolic search is a turning around in a circle, following the shadow cast by the tree through the hours of the day and the seasons of the year. The exterior quest has become an internal obsession; the image of the beloved (*idolo*) is quite literally an idol: "l'idolo mio scolpito in vivo lauro."

In his brilliant article on this sestina, Robert Durling has produced further evidence of the idolatrous quality of its content. It is, he reminds us, an anniversary poem celebrating the poet's meeting with Laura. Since this occurred on Good Friday, a private liturgy of love is here substituted for the liturgy of the cross. Moreover, the laurel, with its branches of diamond, has become an idolatrous cross of glory. In other words, the most significant of Christianity's *signs* has become virtually a proper name. The pun, underscoring the opacity of the sign (*Laura/lauro*), makes any mediation impossible.

There is a further point to be made about this sestina, concerning its last lines:

> L'auro e i topacii al sol sopra la neve
> vincon le bionde chiome presso agli occhi
> che menan gli anni miei sì tosto a riva.

> [Gold and topaz in the sun above the snow are vanquished by the golden locks next to those eyes that lead my years so quickly to shore.]

The comparison of Laura's face to gold and topaz on the snow, sparkling in the sun, is not only reified and coldly beautiful, it is radically fragmentary in a way that scarcely seems accidental. One of the consequences of treating a signifier as an absolute is that its integrity cannot be maintained. Without a principle of intelligibility, a collection of signs threatens to break down into its component parts. To put the matter in medieval terms, we may say that the Spirit is the "form" of the letter in the same way that the soul is the form of the body. In the absence of such a principle of anteriority, signs lose their connection to each other. So it is with Laura. Her virtues and her beauties are scattered like the objects of fetish worship: her eyes and hair are like gold and topaz on the snow, while the outline of her face is lost; her fingers are like ivory and roses or oriental pearls, her eyes are the pole stars, her arms are branches of diamond. Like the poetry that celebrates her, she gains immortality at the price of vitality and historicity. Each part of her has the significance of her entire person; it remains the task of the reader to string together her gemlike qualities into an idealized unity.

The same may be said of the unity of the *Canzoniere*. In order to remove from the poems all traces of temporality and contingency, poetic instants are strung together like pearls on an invisible strand. The lyrics themselves counterfeit a *durée* by their physical proximity and so create a symbolic time, free of the threat of closure. The arrangement of these *rime sparse,* whatever its rationale, may be thought of as an attempt to spatialize time and so to introduce a narrative element in a way that does not threaten to exceed the carefully delimited confines of the text. It is reminiscent to us of cinematographic art, a counterfeit of time wherein a series of images are spatially juxtaposed, awaiting a temporality that will give them life from the outside. Since Petrarch's day, the strategy has been used by innumerable authors of sonnet-sequences, so that it remains one of the most familiar devices of literary self-portraiture.

I have spoken repeatedly of Petrarch's *attempt* to exclude referentiality from his text. His success, of course, was only relative. Not only is referentiality intrinsic to all language, but also there towered behind him the figure of Dante, to whom all love poetry, especially in Italian, would forever after be referred, if only by contrast. Beatrice is in many senses the opposite of Laura. She was a mediatrix, continually pointing beyond herself to God. Throughout most of the *Paradiso,* for example, the pilgrim looks to her eyes only obliquely so that he sees what lies beyond her. Laura's eyes, by contrast, are "homicidal mirrors" in which her narcissistic lover finds spiritual death. When we translate that theme into poetic terms, we conclude that the lady celebrated by Petrarch is a brilliant surface, a pure signifier whose momentary exteriority to the poet serves as an Archimedean point from which he can create himself.

One of the Dantesque themes that most clearly suggests Beatrice's epistemological function as a sign is the theme of her veil, used extensively in the last cantos of the *Purgatorio.* Her unveiling of her face is peculiarly apt to illustrate the parallelism of language and desire in the Augustinian tradition, for the motif is at once erotic and semiotic: her feminine beauty *revealed* within the context of an intellectual and doctrinal *re-velation.* In the canto of the Medusa (*Inf.* 9.63: "Sotto il velame de li versi strani"), Dante had already referred to the significance of his poem with the same figure: his verses were a *veil* to his meaning. It seems likely that in analogous passages, most notably that of the Siren (*Purg.* 19.63), we are meant to perceive this metalinguistic dimension of meaning. Even in our own day the figure is still used to describe the process of representation. C. S. Peirce, in the passage cited above, makes suggestive use of it: "The meaning of a representation can be nothing but a representation. In fact, it is nothing but the representation itself conceived as stripped of irrelevant clothing. But this clothing can never be completely stripped off; it is only changed for something more diaphanous. So there is an infinite regression here." The Freudian (or neo-Freudian) implications do not concern us here; the point is that from St. Paul to Dante the veil covering a radiant face was used as a figure for the relationship of the sign to its referent. In the light of this tradition, it can hardly be fortuitous that Laura's veil, though also a covering, was at times her only reality.

This is the significance, I believe, of what seems otherwise to be simply a charming madrigal (*Rime 52*):

> Non al suo amante piú Dïana piacque
> quando per tal ventura tutta ignuda
> la vide in mezzo de le gelide acque,
>
> ch'a me la pastorella alpestra et cruda
> posta a bagnar un leggiadretto velo
> ch'a l'aura il vago et biondo capel chiuda;
>
> tal che mi fece, or quand' egli arde 'l cielo,
> tutto tremar d'un amoroso gielo.

[Diana did not so please her lover when, by a similar stroke of fortune, he beheld her completely naked amid the icy waters, as did the cruel alpine shepherdess please me, seated to wash a pretty little veil that protects her [Laura's] lovely blonde hair from the breeze: she made me, now when the summer sky is burning, tremble all over with an amorous chill.]

Laura's name, hidden in the pun of the sixth line, is her only presence in these verses, just as her veil is her only presence in the charming anecdote. Her veil, bathed in the water like the naked goddess seen by Acteon, functions as a fetish, an erotic signifier of a referent whose absence the lover refuses to acknowledge. So poetically, the reified verbal sign, wrenched free of its semantic context (*l'aura*/*Laura*), must be read as an affirmation of poetic presence, the *word* (and by extension the poem) as its own sole and sufficient meaning. For all of its lightheartedness, the poem illustrates the fundamental strategy of the *Canzoniere:* the *thematics* of idolatry transformed into the *poetics* of presence.

I do not mean to imply that the sin of idolatry exhausts the thematics of the *Canzoniere*. Many of the later poems suggest that the love for Laura was ennobling, at least in a literary or humanistic sense. My point is simply that idolatry, however repugnant to an Augustinian moralist, is at the linguistic level the essence of poetic autonomy. Because language and desire are indistinguishable in a literary text, we may say that by accusing his persona of an idolatrous passion Petrarch was affirming his own autonomy as a poetic creator. To psychologize about "spiritual torment" in the *Canzoniere* is to live the illusion that Petrarch was perhaps the first to create.

Many more studies of this length would be required to illustrate the full implications of this affirmation for the history of love poetry. In germ, it suggests that all the fictions of courtly love have their semiotic justifications: the love must be idolatrous for its poetic expression to be autonomous; the idolatry cannot be unconflicted, any more than a sign can be completely nonreferential if it is to communicate anything at all. Spiritual struggle stands for the dialectic of literary creation, somewhere between opaque carnality and transparent transcendency. Finally, it might be suggested that the illicit or even adulterous nature of the passion has its counterpart in the "anxiety of influence": communication demands that our signs be appropriated; poetic creation often requires that they be stolen. Petrarch's prodigious originality is that he was entirely self-conscious about the principles of which his predecessors were only dimly aware. By transforming the Augustinian analysis of sin into a new aesthetic, he made self-alienation in life the mark of self-creation in literature and so established a literary tradition that has yet to be exhausted.

The *Canzoniere* ends with a prayer to the Virgin for forgiveness. Laura, he says, was a Medusa who turned him into a man of stone. Nevertheless, I have shown that the deadend nature of that passion is a sign of the poetry's monumentality. In the same poem, he addresses the Virgin as the antitype of his beloved, affirming that the Queen of Heaven is the only true mediatrix: *vera beatrice*. At one level, of course, his refusal to capitalize that familiar word suggests that Dante too had his problems with idolatry and reification. At another level, however, it identifies his own beloved with that of his literary ancestor. On that ambiguous note, both the passion and the poem are concluded and Petrarchism is born.

GIUSEPPE MAZZOTTA

The Canzoniere *and the Language*
of the Self

It would be difficult to exaggerate the importance of the poet's selfhood in the *Canzoniere*: one might even say that few other poets are as tenaciously intent as Petrarch on making the self the locus of singular and significant experiences and so obsessively bent on registering its variable moods. Critics have long spoken of Petrarch's humanism and modernity precisely in terms of his discovery of the centrality of the self: this self appears, as they have acknowledged, fragmented, wounded in his will; or, as the poet himself writes, alluding to his moral drama, "et veggio il meglio et al peggior m'appiglio [and I see the better but I lay hold on the worse]" (264.136).

The status of the moral dilemma, which is suggested by this line and which demonstrably punctuates the *Canzoniere,* is by no means clear in the economy of the text. There are critics who have dismissed the value of the moral language or, a priori, reduced it to a symbolic function, a formal element in the esthetics of pure poetry which Petrarch, as a Mallarmé *avant la lettre,* entertained as his fundamental project. One might object, however, that there seems to be a sense in which Petrarch would certainly want us to believe in the authenticity and exemplary character of his moral experience. The very first sonnet of the *Canzoniere* comes forth as a palinode, a deliberate self-staging in which the poet, on the face of it, speaks with a voice of moral authority, the voice of a public self who finally confesses his past errors and disavows them.

From *Studies in Philology* 75, no. 3 (Summer 1978). © 1978 by the University of North Carolina Press.

With a few exceptions, critics have been alert to the extended ironies that disrupt the notion that the *Canzoniere* is the poetic narrative of a conversion, the moral account, that is, of the experience of a poet who has finally reached the vantage point from which a structure of intelligibility can be imposed on the temporal fragmentation of the self. The first palinodic sonnet, for instance, recalls the last canzone to the Virgin. The implied link between beginning and end gives the poetic sequence a circular structure which challenges the possibility of renewal and leads the reader to suspect that the moral claim is the ambiguous expedient by which the poet attempts to constitute his own self as an "authority."

Faced with these poetic and moral ambiguities (of which the recurrent pattern of antitheses and the oxymora are transparent stylistic emblems), other critics read the *Canzoniere* as the account of the poet's deeply divided mind, caught in the fallen world of nature, unable or unwilling to reach grace, and seeking an esthetic redemption. The *Canzoniere* is thus viewed as a narcissistic and idolatrous construct because it tells the story of a poet who loves the work of his own hands and manufactures his own grace. The "fama" or the laurel tree which Petrarch relentlessly sought is seen as the humanistic and idolatrous simulacrum of Christian eternity.

All of these critical perspectives share the sense that the poetic text is the ground for the constitution of the self: this may be a moral, idolatrous, or esthetic self, but it is one that occupies an unquestionable centrality in his poetic discourse. The poet, it would seem, is certainly involved in a world of mortality and time but poetry is the act which reduces his shifting, fragmented existence into manageable disguises of order and unity. Gianfranco Contini refers to the *Canzoniere* as precisely the attempt to unify experience; and, by a deliberately formulaic turn of phrase, he defines it as the place where "romantic" oscillations and moods are disciplined by a counterpoint of formal "classical" order. On the other hand, when the fragmentary character of the text is stressed, critics will account for it by a curious but common extratextual detour rather than by an analysis of the poetic mechanism at work. Making use of an essentially Petrarchan scheme of historical periodization, they place Petrarch at the center, at the critical crossroads where a medieval view of the cosmos, sustained by principles of hierarchy and order, gives way to the new humanistic age which he heralded and forged. In this new age, there is no certainty in a Logos that may gather together the shattered pieces of experience, and traditional perspectives of moral order have lost their vital applicability.

Yet Petrarch seems to call into question in the *Canzoniere,* as I plan to show in the following pages, precisely the myth of the center and of the centrality of the self. My exegetical effort will be directed not so much at contradicting previous critical views as at redefining terms such as the self, its unity and presence, in what might be called Petrarch's poetics of fragmentation. My point of departure will be a close examination of a few poems in which the paradigm of the self is made much of (the myths of Narcissus and Acteon particularly). Memory, imagination and desire, the terms within which the poet's act of self-making is carried out, appear to be ambiguous instruments of the poetic project. The second part of the paper will explore Petrarch's sense of this ambiguity, his intuition that the constitutive ambiguity of poetic language blurs any explicit thematic formulation. It is undeniable, for instance, that at an explicit thematic level, Petrarch oscillates between idolatry and conversion. Idolatry and conversion, however, are both postures by which he attempts to charge the elusive and deluding nature of language with a substantiality that language can never achieve. The ambiguities of the *Canzoniere* are of a moral order only in a secondary sense: this does not mean that they can be dismissed as simple accessories to the poetic nucleus, as Noferi suggests; they are secondary because they depend on the knowledge that the self, in the mirror of self-reflection—as he is the object of his own thoughts—can never coincide with his own specular images.

Along with my concern to show the insufficiency of thematic criticism, I also wish to suggest some traits of Petrarch's lyrical voice. I ought to remark at the outset that the conventional judgment on his lyric is still well within the bounds of De Sanctis's evaluation: when Petrarch is not too deliberate and indulgently self-conscious, as is occasionally the case, he is considered a truly lyrical poet. The lyric emerges as the conventional privileged form of literary discourse because it is the representation of the will and the direct and spontaneous expression of the self: Laura may be absent, but the voice of the poet is always present to relieve the grief because, as Petrarch himself has it, "cantando il duol si disacerba [singing to assuage the pain]" (30.4).

Sonnet 90 has conventionally been read as a specimen of genuine lyrical self-expression. In it, Laura's past beauty—as Noferi argues in her extensive analysis—is recovered and transfigured in the "absolute space" that the poem manages to evoke:

> Erano i capei d'oro a l'aura sparsi
> che 'n mille dolci nodi gli avolgea,

e il vago lume oltre misura ardea
di quei begli occhi, ch'or ne son sì scarsi;

e il viso di pietosi color farsi,
non so se vero o falso mi parea:
i' che l'esca amorosa al petto avea,
qual meraviglia se di subito arsi?

Non era l'andar suo cosa mortale,
ma d'angelica forma; et le parole
sonavan altro, che pur voce umana.

Uno spirto celeste, un vivo sole
fu quel ch'i' vidi: et se non fosse or tale,
piaga per allentar d'arco non sana.

[Her golden hair was loosed to the breeze, which turned it in a
thousand sweet knots, and the lovely light burned without
measure in her eyes, which are now so stingy of it; and it
seemed to me (I know not whether truly or falsely) her face
took on the color of pity: I, who had the tinder of love in my
breast, what wonder is it if I suddenly caught fire? Her walk
was not that of a mortal thing but of some angelic form, and
her words sounded different from a merely human voice: a
celestial spirit, a living sun was what I saw, and if she were not
such now, a wound is not healed by the loosening of the bow.]

The sonnet is articulated, quite clearly, on a temporal antithesis, the *then*
of the vision and the present ravages of time on Laura: the antithesis
introduces and stresses the persistence of the poet's memory and his love.
The poet's memory, in a real sense, is the privileged metaphor: by it, the
sonnet seems to move toward transcending the flow of time, toward
preserving inviolate—by the esthetic transfiguration—the image of Laura;
at the same time, memory is the metaphor which engenders the poet's
stability and gives continuity to his own temporal experience. Now, as
then, the concluding phrase implies, the wound produced by the arrows of
love in the poet goes on bleeding.

We must look more closely at the poem, however, to discover the
complications of this explicit thematic thrust. The metaphor of the "esca
amorosa" (l. 7) by which the lover is trapped in the snares of love is
strongly reminiscent of Andreas Capellanus's definition of love. In *De Arte
Honeste Amandi,* partly following the etymology canonized by Isidore of

Seville, Andreas derives the word *amor* from *hamus,* because by it man is "hooked," chained by desire. The metaphor he uses is that of the shrewd fisherman who uses bait to catch fish, or, as a fourteenth-century Italian translation of *De Arte* renders it, "'colui che ama, dalli uncini della concupiscenza é preso e disidera di prendere l'altro col suo amo, siccome il pescatore savio s'ingegna coll'eschette di trarre li pesci [he who loves is caught by the hooks of concupiscence and the desire to take the other with his love, since the wise fisherman does his best to draw in fish with bait].'' Andreas's chains are chains of cupidity; Petrarch, on the contrary, suspends the erotic charge of the allusion within a distinctly stilnovistic rhetoric.

As has been widely acknowledged, the sonnet echoes both Dante's "Tanto gentile" and Guinizzelli's "Io voglio del ver." The stilnovists, to be sure, burden the appearance of the lady with a sense of moral illumination, but Petrarch rescues their language from definite moral overtones and deploys it so as to transfigure the image of Laura within a magic timelessness. We should not see in the conflation of the courtly motif and stilnovistic resonances simply an instance of Petrarch's dualism, his ambiguous view of the lady who is partly "donna angelicata," partly object of erotic desire. Much as for Dante in "Tanto gentile," so for Petrarch the celebration of Laura's otherworldly beauty is the pretext for raising what is perhaps the fundamental question of the sonnet, the meaning of appearance.

The metaphor of appearance is introduced in the opening two lines of the sonnet. It has been suggested that these lines are patterned on Virgil's description of the vision of Venus in the *Aeneid* ("dederatque comam diffundere ventis [and she had given her hair to the disheveling wind]") and the Ovidian myth of Daphne ("et levis impulsos retro dabat aura capillos [and a light air flung her locks streaming behind her].") But these reminiscences, I would submit, cluster about a closer parallel which occurs in Ovid's description of Diana in the *Metamorphoses*. The goddess, attended by her nymphs, prepares to bathe: one nymph takes the bow, another the robe, the defter of them "*sparsos* per colla *capillos conligit in nodum* [binds into a knot the locks which have fallen down her . . . neck]," a line which is verbally echoed and woven into Petrarch's "erano i *capei* d'oro a l'aura *sparsi* / che 'n mille dolci *nodi* gli *avolgea*." Characteristically, Petrarch draws what Ovid describes as the action of the nymph on Diana into a solipsistic and self-reflexive circle: it is the "aura" which ties Laura's hair in a thousand curls. Ovid's myth, as we shall see later on, deals largely with Acteon's glance which violates the nakedness of Diana as he looks into that which should remain invisible and is subsequently transformed into a stag.

Like the stilnovistic allusion, the Ovidian echoes celebrate Laura's epiphany as a visionary experience bordering on the phantasmatic; but—paradoxically—she is absent from the sonnet. The pun "l'aura" (l. 1) is both the stylized *senhal* for Laura and the sign of her elusiveness. This elusiveness occurs at the heart of the vision: she appears, in a real sense, by being invisible, as "uno spirto celeste, un vivo sole" (l. 12), emblems that imply transparency or light which in its excess dazzles and blinds. Her very face, like the sound of her words, is defined ambiguously "non so se vero or falso mi parea" (l. 6). The deceptiveness depends, no doubt, on the divine and human attributes of the image. But more is implied. For Petrarch, the very nature of the appearance of the image is for it to be unsettling, with its contours blurred.

By the act of memory, the poet tries to give Laura's apparition a stabilized and fixed presence that may redeem and abolish time; but the image cannot be deciphered. More importantly, the act of memory dislodges the poet into a disorienting space where the reality of Laura's decline ("begli occhi, ch'*or* ne son sì scarsi," l. 4) is suspended into an hypothesis. The concluding lines of the sonnet, "et se non fosse *or* tale / piaga per allentar d'arco non sana" (ll. 13–14), by their hypothetical structure throw into doubt the reality of the present time. The poet's memory, then, far from being simply a stabilizing metaphor, manifests itself both as the illusory act of the mind to establish a temporal continuity and as the fiction which threatens the poet's sense of time and his stance.

But the poet is threatened in a more radical way. The vision of Laura which binds his will and from which there is no escaping is obliquely cast in terms of a specifically poetic danger, namely, the danger of losing the poetic voice. In Dante's "Tanto gentile," at the appearance of Beatrice "ogni lingua deven tremando muta [each tongue, trembling, becomes mute]" and, as in Guinizzelli's "Io voglio del vero," the poet can only praise the lady's virtues. In the Ovidian tale, on the other hand, Acteon sees Diana and loses his voice: "nunc tibi me posito visam velamine narres / si poteris narrare licet [now you are free to tell that you have seen me all unrobed, if you can tell]." His loss of voice is the consequence of his moral transgression. For Petrarch, by these oblique allusions, what seems to be a spontaneous experience of lyrical self-expression is ironically reversed into an awareness of a poetic crisis which depends on the unsettling nature of the imaginary experience.

In the only sonnet where the myth of Narcissus is explicitly recalled,

Petrarch explores precisely the dangers of the imaginary experience. Paradoxically, the myth is applied to Laura, not to the poet; the sonnet (45), in fact, focuses on her as she sees herself reflected in the mirror and is absorbed in a narcissistic self-love.

> Il mio adversario in cui veder solete
> gli occhi vostri che Amor e 'l cielo honora,
> colle non sue bellezze v'innamora
> più che 'n guisa mortal soavi e liete.
>
> Per consiglio di lui, donna, m'avete
> scacciato dal mio dolce albergo fora:
> misero exilio, avegna ch'i' non fora
> d'abitar degno over voi sola siete.
>
> Ma s'io v'era con saldi chiovi fisso,
> non devea specchio farvi per mio danno,
> a voi stessa piacendo, aspra et superba.
>
> Certo se vi rimembra di Narcisso,
> questo et quel corso ad un termino vanno,
> benché di sí bel fior sia indegna l'erba.

[My adversary in whom you are wont to see your eyes, which Love and Heaven honor, enamors you with beauties not his but sweet and happy beyond mortal guise. By his counsel, Lady, you have driven me out of my sweet dwelling: miserable exile! even though I may not be worthy to dwell where you alone are. But if I had been nailed there firmly, a mirror should not have made you, because you pleased yourself, harsh and proud to my harm. Certainly, if you remember Narcissus, this and that course lead to one goal—although the grass is unworthy of so lovely a flower.]

The mirror has seduced Laura and is thus the rival of the lover: described in terms of negativity and emptiness at the beginning of the poem ("colle non sue bellezze," l. 3), it acquires in the second stanza a definite substantiality as it insidiously charms Laura to cast the lover into exile. Discreetly, the mirror is alluded to as a kind of *losengier*. In the poetry of both trouvères and troubadours, the losengier is the deceiving and inimical talebearer who insinuates himself into the lady's graces, flatters her and displaces the true lover. In the troubadoric love drama, the losengier plays the role of the voyeur whose eyes violate any secrecy; for Petrarch, it becomes a purely imaginary and fictive self-projection. Like a losengier, the mirror flatters and separates the lover from Laura and, by a dramatic twist, Petrarch exposes the narcissistic basis of troubador poetry as he shows that the blandishments of the losengier are a mere self-gratifying reflection leading to harshness and self-love (l. 11).

The sonnet ends with an allusion to Narcissus and his death. Laura is in the presence of her own image, and the poet reminds Laura, locked in her erotic self-reification, that the coincidence of self and self's image is nothing less than Narcissus's experience of death. The allusion to the Ovidian myth of Narcissus is more than a simple metaphoric correlation or a reference of merely historical interest: by recalling the story from the *Metamorphoses*, Petrarch undertakes a reading which is startlingly profound.

Narcissus, in Ovid's story, can live only if he will never know himself— such was the promise of the gods. The youth dies at the fountain when he has known himself, when he has seen, that is to say, his own image and has discovered its emptiness. He sees first the emptiness of the shadow he loves ("*nihil* habet ista *sui* [(it) has no substance of its own]" is the lament and Petrarch seems to echo it in the phrase "non sue belleze") and then discovers that he is that empty shadow: "iste ego sum [I am he]." The conceptual implication of the story is clear: whatever authentic self-knowledge is possible, it is equivalent to death. Or, what amounts to the same thing, death is the knowledge of one's own vanity.

The idolatrous self-love of Narcissus is the tragedy of self-knowledge, the unbearable experience of facing one's own finitude. At the same time, the imaginary self-representation emerges as the locus of death. But Petrarch alludes to Narcissus and moves well beyond the moment of his death. The metaphor of the metamorphosis, on which he insists in the last three lines of the sonnet, implies that the coincidence between the self and its image is illusory. It also spells out the fact that Narcissus after death is displaced into a radical otherness: as he is metamorphosed into a flower, the flower is caught in the world of temporality and imperma-nence where it will live by continuously dying. Metamorphosis is for Petrarch the metaphor of spatial and temporal dislocation, the hint that no form is ever stable and that every form is always moving toward still other forms.

The analogy between Narcissus and Laura, which is the burden of the last tercet, carries with it the implication that Laura, too, is threatened with the same displacement that Narcissus experienced. Yet the last line "benché di sí bel fior sia indegna l'erba" subverts the analogy. We should perhaps remark that we are dealing here with a common rhetorical feature of Petrarch's poetry, one which was most fruitfully picked up, for instance, by Leopardi. An analogy is set up between two terms but the movement of the poem finally denies the posited correspondence. Leopardi deploys this technique constantly: in "Canto notturno d'un pastore errante dell'Asia," to give one example, a resemblance between the moon and the shepherd "somiglia alla tua vita / la vita del pastore [resembles to your life the life of the shepherd]" is established. The articulation of the poem, however, shows the analogy to be the poet's wistful impulse to find significant bonds between the self and what the self is not. The analogy is finally demystified and its terms return to their original disjunction.

In Petrarch's sonnet, the collapse of the analogy between Narcissus and Laura seems, on the surface, to function as a mildly hyperbolic device to insinuate the notion of Laura's singularity and the praise of her beauty. The seemingly conventional and innocuous tribute hides, however, a less reassuring and less bland meaning. It does not do violence to the text to read the distinction of Laura from Narcissus as a suggestion that Laura will be displaced like Narcissus, but unlike him, she will belong literally nowhere: she will be a purely imaginary flower and will exist in the non-place of the imagination. The detail of the unworthiness of the grass to bear and contain Laura subtly alludes to the poet's own unworthiness "avvegna ch'i' non forza / d'abitar *degno* ove voi sola siete" (ll. 7–8). The dislocation is total: Narcissus is a flower, Laura is in the utopian domain of the imaginary, the poet is in his exile. Petrarch, as we know, gives thematic weight to the question of exile: the lover is always distant, always somewhere else, forever seeking the time and space of his encounter with Laura. Distance, in this sense, is essential to desire, for it allows desire to exist as a perennial tension. But dislocation exceeds the thematic notion of loss of space and involves, as we shall presently see, the very conditions of figurative language.

In both the sonnets that we have examined, the image elicited by memory or reflected by the mirror, far from being a stable and idolatrous sign for the self, endangers the sense of selfhood. In Sonnet 45, as Laura is provisionally related to Narcissus, the poet is Echo, an emblem of the disembodied voice alluding to its own hollowness. The myth of Acteon, which reappears in a short poem (52), goes even further and exemplifies the dislocation of the poetic voice as an involuntary experience.

> Non al suo amante più Diana piacque,
> quando per tal ventura tutta ignuda
> la vide in mezzo de la gelide acque,

ch'a me la pastorella alpestre e cruda
posta a bagnar un leggiadretto velo,
che a l'aura il vago e biondo capel chiuda,

tal che mi fece, or quand'egli arde il cielo
tutto tremar d'un amoroso gielo.

[Not so much did Diana please her lover when, by a similar
chance, he saw her all naked amid the icy waters, as did the
cruel mountain shepherdess please me, set to wash a pretty veil
that keeps her lovely blond head from the breeze; so that she
made me, even now when the sky is burning, all tremble with a
chill of love.]

The madrigal has a deceptive pastoral simplicity: ostensibly it is built on a
comparison between Acteon's pleasure at seeing Diana bathing naked and
the poet's own pleasure at seeing a shepherdess washing a veil which will
tie Laura's hair. Unified by metaphors of bathing (Diana's ablutions and
the veil's being washed), rhyme and internal assonances (quando . . .
biondo . . . quando), the madrigal attempts to capture a sense of harmoni-
ous pastoral order and moves toward the conventional cliché of the final
line, the antithesis of ice and fire.

The myth of Diana is once again recalled but this time from Acteon's
point of view. Acteon is like the poet and, in effect, he is the metaphor for
the poet, the voyeur who sees unseen Diana's nakedness and transgresses
the bounds of the sacred space that must remain inaccessible to him. As
Petrarch alludes to the myth, however, he simultaneously eludes it. The
strategy of the transition from Acteon to the poet's experience is remarkable: it is as if in the empty space that separates the two tercets, Petrarch
turns his eyes away and blinds himself to the possibility of violation.

A chain of metaphoric dislocations from the erotic scene of Diana is
thus set in motion. Whereas Acteon sees the naked Diana who in Ovid's
language was "posito visam velamine [you have seen (me) unrobed],"
Petrarch picks up the veil and covers that nakedness. The sequence of
images, the shepherdess who washes the veil that will tie the hair of Laura
(herself, once again, alluded to and eluded by the pun "l'aura") bears a
tenuous relation to the myth. There is no necessary link between the two
experiences: Petrarch domesticates the scene as he evokes Acteon's
encounter. The diminutives "pastorella" "leggiadretto" conjure up a pastoral world (and the madrigal is the poetic form of the pastoral) which
shelters the self from the tragic possibilities of the myth, what in Canzone

23 is referred to as a veritable loss of one's own image (ll. 155ff.).

The final phrase of the madrigal, "tutto tremar d'un amoroso gielo," ostensibly makes the self the endpoint of the sequence of dislocations, and suggests how the poem moves toward the constitution of the self as a center of perception. But the phrase circles back to the opening description of Diana "*tutta* ignuda in mezzo de le *gelide* acque." If the analogy between Acteon and the poet collapses as the poet does not look at the goddess, he now insinuates that he is like Diana. The shift of perspective is hardly surprising in Petrarch's poetry: he often casts himself, as is well known, in the role of Apollo and, in the same breath, casts Laura as the sun. The shift implies that the categories of subject and object are precarious and reversible. More fundamentally, the shift insinuates a doubleness at the moment in which the selfhood is constituted: Petrarch is at the same time both Acteon and Diana but he is also neither, a double, like the two foci of an ellipsis always implicating each other and always apart.

It is in this space of the elliptical movement that the metaphoric circulation of Petrarch's poetry is woven. In all three poems so far considered, at the moment of resolution each poem changes its direction and returns on itself to some other textual point insofar as its thematic sense is reversed and other hidden perspectives emerge. These perspectives are by no means hidden, they are rather the surface of the text in the sense that for Petrarch the text is always by necessity the surface. The prominent figure in madrigal 52 is precisely the veil which Diana has put aside and Petrarch stretches over her nakedness. The veil, the metaphor that makes the difference between the experience of Acteon and the poet's, is involuntary. The phrase "per tal ventura" (l. 2)—which directly echoes Ovid's sense of the fortuitousness of Acteon's vision of Diana ("at bene si quaeras, *fortunae* crimen illo, non scelus invenies [but if you seek the truth you will find the cause of this in fortune's fault, and not in any crime of his]")— carries a special force in the madrigal. It is the contingency of the encounter, the involuntary experience that Petrarch stresses. We know that he frequently validates the involuntary events: in the third sonnet, for instance, he becomes a *captivus amoris* when he is "senza sospetto . . . del tutto disarmato." The willed efforts generate illusory epiphanies while the involuntary encounters are essential and significant. In a general sense, this is Petrarch's critique of the inadequacy of the will, the ironic awareness that his love quest is doomed to fail. More particularly, the phrase "per tal ventura" implies that the emergence of the veil lies beyond his will, that the dislocation which his own metaphors figure is involuntary. The poet's deliberate attempt to construct the self, to set up analogies by which the

self is constituted, is obfuscated by the veil. But what does it mean to say
that the veil is involuntary and what does the veil—a term deeply charged
with allegorical resonances—mask? We must look closely at Canzone 125
where Petrarch grounds his notion of the self and its elusiveness within the
larger questions of language and desire.

> Se 'l pensier che mi strugge,
> com'è pungente et saldo,
> così vestisse d'un color conforme,
> forse tal m'arde et fugge,
> ch'avria parte del caldo,
> et desteriasi Amor là dov'or dorme;
> men solitarie l'orme
> foran de' miei pie' lassi
> per campagne et per colli,
> ardendo lei che come un ghiaccio stassi,
> et non lascia in me dramma
> che non sia foco et fiamma.
>
> Però ch'Amor mi sforza
> et di saver mi spoglia,
> parlo in rime aspre et di dolcezze ignude:
> Ma non sempre a la scorza
> ramo, né in fior, né 'n foglia,
> mostra di for sua natural vertude.
> Miri ciò che 'l cor chiude,
> Amor et que' begli occhi,
> ove si siede a l'ombra.
> Se 'l dolor che si sgombra
> avèn che 'n pianto o in lamentar trabocchi,
> l'un a me noce, et l'altro
> altrui, ch'io non lo scaltro.
>
> Dolci rime leggiadre
> che nel primiero assalto
> d'Amor usai, quand'io non ebbi altr'arme,
> chi verrà mai che squadre
> questo mi cor di smalto
> ch'almen, com'io solea, possa sfogarme?
> Ch'aver dentro a lui parme
> un che madonna sempre

depinge et de lei parla:
a voler poi ritrarla,
per me non basto; e par ch'io me ne stempre.
Lasso!, così m'è scorso
lo mio dolce soccorso.

Come fanciul ch'a pena
volge la lingua et snoda,
che dir non sa, ma 'l più tacer gli è noia,
così 'l desir mi mena
a dire; et vo' che m'oda
la dolce mia nemica anzi ch'io moia.
Se forse ogni sua gioia
nel suo bel viso è solo,
et di tutt'altro è schiva,
odil tu, verde riva,
et presta a' miei sospir sì largo volo,
che sempre si ridica
come tu m'eri amica.

Ben sai che sì bel piede
non toccò terra unquancho
come quel dì che già segnata fosti;
onde il cor lasso riede,
col tormentoso fianco,
a partir teco i lor pensier nascosti.
Così avestù riposti
de' be' vestigi sparsi
anchor tra' fiori et l'erba,
che la mia vita acerba,
lagrimando, trovasse ove acquetarsi!
Ma come pò s'appaga
l'alma dubbiosa et vaga.

Ovunque gli occhi volgo
trovo un dolce sereno
pensando: qui percosse il vago lume.
Qualunque herba o fior colgo
credo che nel terreno
aggia radice, ov'ella ebbe in costume
gir fra le piagge e 'l fiume,

et talor farsi un seggio
fresco, fiorito et verde.
Così nulla sen perde;
et più certezza averne fora il peggio.
Spirto beato, quale
se', quando altrui fai tale?

O poverella mia, come se' rozza!
Credo che tel conoschi:
rimanti in questi boschi.

[If the care that torments me, as it is sharp and dense, so were
clothed in a conformable color, perhaps one burns me and flees
who would have part of the heat, and Love would awaken
where now he is sleeping; less solitary would be the prints of
my weary feet through fields and across hills, my eyes less wet
always: if she were aflame who now stands like ice and leaves
not a dram in me that is not fire and flame. Since Love forces
me and strips me of all skill, I speak in harsh rhymes naked of
sweetness; but not always does a branch show forth its natural
virtue in flower or in leaf. Let Love and those lovely eyes,
where he is sitting in the shade, look on what my heart has shut
up in itself. If my sorrow which unburdens itself happens to
overflow in weeping or lamenting, the one pains me and the
other pains someone else, for I do not polish it. Sweet graceful
rhymes that I used in the first assault of Love, when I had no
other arms: who will ever come who can shatter the stone
about my heart, so that at least I can pour myself forth as I
used to do? for it seems to me that I have someone within who
always portrays my lady and speaks of her: I am not sufficient
to describe her by myself, and I come untuned because of it;
alas, so has my sweet comfort fled! Like a child who can hardly
move and untangle his tongue, who is not able to speak but
hates to be silent any longer, thus desire leads me to speak, and
I wish my sweet enemy to hear me before I die. If, perhaps, she
takes joy only in her lovely face and flees everything else, do
you, green shore, hear it and lend to my sighs so wide a flight
that it be always remembered that you were kind to me. You
know well that so beautiful a foot never touched the earth as
on that day when you were marked by hers, wherefore my
weary heart comes back with my tormented flanks to share

with you their hidden cares. Would you had hidden away some lovely footprints still among the flowers and grass, that my bitter life might weeping find a place to become calm! but my fearful, yearning soul satisfies itself as best it can. Wherever I turn my eyes, I find a sweet brightness, thinking: "Here fell the bright light of her eyes." Whatever grass or flower I gather, I believe that it is rooted in the ground where she was wont to walk through the meadows beside the river, and sometimes to make herself a seat, fresh, flowering, and green. Thus no part is omitted and to know more exactly would be a loss. Blessed spirit, what are you if you make another become such? O poor little song, how inelegant you are! I think you know it: stay here in these woods.]

The poet starts by recalling his exile from Laura: cast in the form of a *planctus*, the poem dramatizes the poet's lonely wanderings (ll. 5–7) in an open and unbounded landscape as a veritable quest which culminates in the last stanza (ll. 66–78). Laura is nowhere in the poem and the quest, in effect, is not for Laura but for her vestiges (ll. 60–63) which might allay the restlessness of the lover's heart. The landscape does not preserve her vestiges and the poet recoils into a deliberate self-mystification: he acknowledges as illusory the space, the "qui" of her presence, for "como puó s'appaga / l'alma dubbiosa et vaga" (ll. 64–65).

This quest for the signs of Laura, which ends by exposing the self-mystification as the presence of a nothingness, masks and hides another more painful and insoluble quest, the poet's quest for poetic language, for the signs that might be adequate to the poet's inner thoughts and such that they may awaken Laura's love from its slumber (ll. 3–5). Seen in this perspective, the canzone is a veritable grammar of styles, an inventory of poetic possibilities. The two stylistic poles within which Petrarch moves, the "rime aspre et di dolcezze ignude" (l. 16) and the "dolci rime leggiadre che nel primiero assalto / d'amor usai" (ll. 27–29), are definite echoes from the canzone in the fourth treatise of the *Convivio*, "Le dolci rime d'amor ch'io solia [The sweet rhymes of love that I am accustomed to sing]." In this allegorical poem in which Dante raises the question of the origin and nature of authority, he leaves behind the "dolci rime" and promises to use "rima aspr'e sottile" as stylistic correlatives adequate to philosophical speculation. Petrarch inverts the terms: possessed by the "rime aspre" which he would leave behind, he recalls the "dolci rime" of the past. We shall see later on the crucial importance of Petrarch's allusion to the allegorical poem of the *Convivio,* for it is a part of a more complex polemic that Petrarch undertakes against Dante.

The first stanza, for instance, ends with a rhyme scheme "et non lascia in me *dramma* / che non sia foco et *fiamma*" (ll. 12–13) which partially picks up the rhyme scheme employed by Dante in the earthly Paradise: "men che *dramma* / di sangue m'è rimaso che non tremi; / conosco i segni dell'antica *fiamma* [not a drop of blood is left in me that does not tremble: I know the tokens of the ancient flame]" (*Purg.* 30.46–48). For Dante this is the juncture where Virgil disappears and the poet finally meets Beatrice. The irony of the allusion is transparent: the dramatic point at which Dante reaches Beatrice in the pastoral world of Eden marks the beginning of Petrarch's own quest for Laura whom he will find only in the illusory garden of the mind. But the irony goes further than this. Dante abandons Virgil, and the translation of the Virgilian line which results ("agnosco veteris vestigia flammae [I recognize the signs of the old flame]" (*Aeneid* 4.23) is a veritable metaphor which stresses Dante's poetic autonomy from his guide. The line which in its original context describes the suicidal and annihilating love of Dido is turned against Virgil to dramatize the pilgrim's and the poet's spiritual resurrection. Petrarch will also attempt to free himself from the specter of Dante.

Canzone 125 is replete with other allusions to the *rime petrose.* Most notably, the lines "chi verrá mai che squadre / questo mio cor di smalto" (ll. 30–31) are a direct paraphrase of two lines in "Così nel mio parlar voglio esser aspro": "fender per mezzo lo core a la crudele che il mio squadra" (ll. 53–54). Even the rhyme scheme "scorza—forza" (ll. 25–26) in "Così nel mio parlar" is inverted as "sforza—scorza" (ll. 14–17) in Petrarch's canzone.

What purpose do these reminiscences from "Così nel mio parlar" serve in the economy of Petrarch's poem? Dante's song describes both his love for the so-called Donna Pietra as an experience of spiritual degradation which threatens to transform the lover into a stone and his attempt to write in a style which is commensurate with the harshness of his own erotic fall:

> Non trovo scudo ch'ella non mi spezzi
> nè loco che dal suo viso m'asconda:
> che come fior di fronda,
> così de la mia mente tien la cima. . . .
> e il peso che m'affonda
> è tal che non potrebbe adequar rima.

[I find no shield that she may not shatter nor place that may
hide me from her sight: but, as a flower the tip of a plant, so of
my mind she holds the summit ... and the weight that is
sinking me is such that no rhyme can equal it.]

(14–17; 20–21)

This love occupies "de la mia mente, ... la cima": the phrase actually
translates the technical *apex mentis* and implies the absolute corruption of
the intellect or, since *mens* is the faculty of intellectual vision, the darken-
ing of reason by the sight of the Medusa.

The first two lines of the stanza enact precisely an allusion to the
myth of the Medusa threatening the unshielded lover who is, in turn, cast
as an unsuccessful Perseus. More importantly, the dramatic process of the
stanza hinges on the coherently related allusion to the Medusa and the
poet's misdirected love defined as a weight that pulls the lover downward
(ll. 20–21). Dante uses an unequivocally Augustinian doctrine of love.
Love, for Augustine, is a metaphoric pull of gravity, the inner weight that
urges the soul to seek its own place. This doctrine, known as *pondus amoris,*
is illustrated by the natural movement of stone and fire. The fire designates
the spiritual ascent; the stone, the erotic fall. Augustine's metaphors are
recalled by Dante: the "peso che m'affonda" is the downward *pondus* of
the stone, the Donna Pietra-Medusa which reduces the lover into a stone.

Petrarch certainly accepts this view of desire as the metaphor of
dislocation: the exile of the lover dramatizes precisely his displacement.
Yet, by coupling the "rime aspre" of the philosophical poem with the
"parlar ... aspro" of "Così nel mio parlar" where the dark eros abrogates
the power of the intellect, he draws attention to the contradictions of
Dante's theory of poetic styles. Petrarch achieves this by using Augustine's
theory of language against Dante.

If the first two stanzas of Song 125 are charged with allusions to
Dante, the third stanza is the turning point away from Dante to Augustine's theory of language and desire.

> Come fanciul ch'a pena
> volge la lingua e snoda
> che dire non sa, ma più il tacer gli è noia
> così il desir mi mena
> a dir.

[Like a child who can hardly move and untangle his tongue,
who is not able to speak but hates to be silent any longer, thus
desire leads me to speak].

The explicit claim that language is rooted in desire is cast in the terminology of Augustine's *Confessions*. This spiritual autobiography, which is in a fundamental way a quest for language, focuses on the *paideia* of a rhetorician and "salesman of words" who, through complex intellectual temptations, gives up the duplicity of rhetoric and turns to the Logos made flesh. Augustine begins by recounting his childhood, the *infantia* (which should be taken with its full etymological sense of speechlessness), and elaborates his theory of signs and language. Language and desire are inextricably bound together: as Augustine will find out in his reading of the Virgilian Dido, language engenders desire, and it originates in desire:

> Quis me commemorat peccatum infantiae meae—quonian nemo mundus a peccato coram te, nec infans, cuius est unius diei vita super terram—quis me commemorat? . . . Quid ergo tunc peccabam? . . . Vidi ergo et expertus sum zelantem parvulum: *nondum loquebatur* et intuebatur pallidus amaro aspectu conlactaneum suum . . . Nonne ab infantia huc pergens in pueritiam? non enim eram *infans, qui non farer*, sed etiam puer loquens eram.

> [Who shall bring to my remembrance the sin of my infancy? For in thy sight can no man be clean from his sin; no, not an infant of a day old upon the earth. Who will put me in mind of this? . . . Wherein did I then sin? . . . I myself have seen and observed a little baby to be already jealous; and before it could speak, what an angry and bitter look it would cast at another child that sucked away its milk from it. . . . Growing on from the state of infancy, came I not into my childhood? For an infant I was no longer, that could not speak; seeing now I began to prove a pretty prating boy.]

The fairly close verbal echoes in Petrarch's text ("fanciul . . . che dir non sa" paraphrases both "nondum loquebatur" and "infans qui non farer") disclose his assimilation of the heart of Augustine's concept. The child who cannot speak and cannot be still is the metaphor by which both Augustine and Petrarch make desire the foundation of language. Yet desire, properly speaking, cannot be a foundation, for desire is a pure privation, a lack generated by man's fallen state. Words and signs are generated from this lack, and are hollow dislocations of it: the poet persistently attempts to achieve a formal adequation to desire and persistently fails, because desire, in its uninterrupted movement toward totality, exceeds any formal adequation. For Petrarch, language is the allegory of desire, a veil, not because it hides a moral meaning but because it always says something else.

In the light of this, we can perhaps grasp the reasons for the presence of technical metaphors drawn from the repertory of the language of allegory. The thrust of "Se il pensier che mi strugge" is to find a language that "vestisse d'un color conforme" (l. 3) the lover's inner thoughts. The implication is that style is exterior to the truth, a veil for the inner feelings. If the term "color," furthermore, transparently alludes to the *colores rhetorici,* "vestisse" designates an allegorical *involucrum.* St. Paul refers to the body as a "cloth" for the soul and the Vulgate translates the clothing by "induere." Macrobius, for his part, uses "vestire" as a conventional metaphor to indicate the cover of allegory. Even more cogently, in the lines "ma non sempre a la scorza / ramo, né in fior, né 'n foglia / mostra di fuor sua natural vertude" (ll. 17–19) the word "scorza" translates the technical *cortex,* the bark which in the language of allegory hides and obscures the meaning, the *medulla* within.

The series of oblique allusions to allegory could be extended, but it is the allusion to Dante's allegorical canzone from the *Convivio* that seems especially pertinent. To Dante's seeming belief that language may reach a genuine philosophical knowledge, Petrarch opposes a vision in which the mind is first stifled by love, and then, at the end of the poem, chooses to delude itself. To his faith in the mimetic possibilities of language, Petrarch opposes the notion of a radical inadequacy of language. If allegory for Dante (as Petrarch read him) is the envelope of hidden truth and an instrument of knowledge, for Petrarch it is constitutive of language and marks the distance between desire and its signs.

It falls outside the scope of this paper to show that Dante's conception of the allegory of poets in the *Convivio,* in spite of the lacunae in the text, is much more complex than Petrarch makes it out to be. We must rather stress the necessity of the veil of allegory and the self-mystification in Petrarch's canzone: they are metaphors of a desire which cannot be named. The inadequacy of language is not merely a *topos* of authorial modesty, as the canons of rhetoric explain it; it suggests, rather, the poet's ironic awareness that there is not a proper name for desire. We must not, however, minimize the fact that desire for Petrarch has a name, bears indeed the proper name of Laura:

> Quando io movo i sospiri a chiamar voi
> e 'l nome che nel cor mi scrisse Amore,
> LAUdando s'incomincia udir di fore
> il suon dei primi dolci accenti suoi.

Vostro stato REal, che 'ncontro poi,
radddoppia a l'alta impresa il mio valore;
ma: TAci, grida il fin che farle honore
è d'altri homeri soma che da' tuoi.

Così LAUdare e REverire insegna
la voce stessa, pur ch'altri vi chiami,
O d'ogni reverenza et d'honor degna:

se non che forse Apollo si disdegna
ch'a parlar dei suoi sempre verdi rami
lingua morTAl presumptuosa vegna.

[When I move my sighs to call you and the name that Love
wrote on my heart, the sound of its first sweet accents is heard
without in LAU-ds. Your RE-gal state, which I meet next,
redoubles my strength for the high enterprise, but "TA-lk no
more!" cries the ending, "for to do her honor is a burden
for other shoulders than yours." Thus the word itself teaches
LAU-d and RE-verence, whenever anyone calls you, O Lady
worthy of all reverence and honor; except that perhaps Apollo
is incensed that any mor-TA-l tongue should come presumptu-
ous to speak of his eternally green boughs.]

The existence of a proper name implies the possibility that language has a
proper sense, an univocal literal referent that localizes and fixes upon itself
the infinite disarticulations of desire. The name of Laura seems to function
precisely in this way: the syllables of Laureta are dispersed through
the text (ll. 3, 5, 7 and 9, 14) and, by the dispersion, they sustain the
movement of the poem and serve as a fulcrum to organize and orient the
space of the sonnet. Her name is "proper" in another sense: it contains
and hides within its syllables the great themes of love poetry, praise and
reverence. It might be said, actually, that the sonnet, with its stress on
praise and Apollo's pursuit of Daphne, dramatizes the etymological possibilities of the word "laurus." Isidore of Seville, for instance, explains that
"laurus a verbo laudis dicta . . . hanc arborem Graeci *dafnen* vocant quod
numquam deponat viriditatem [laurel is said to be derived from the word
for praise. The Greeks call this tree 'daphne' because it never loses its
greenness]." Just as for Isidore etymology is the metaphor for a direct and
necessary link between word and referent, it is Petrarch's fiction that a
"proper" relationship exists between the master-word and its textual
disseminations.

But the anagram ironizes the explicit thematic burden of the poem. It implies that words have no preestablished stability, for, by virtue of the anagram, letters can be extrapolated and reassembled at will—and words become generative of all possible other words. The linear sequence of the text is abolished and the text loses its quality of being an ordering of signs, each fixed, distinct, and self-containedly referential. The property of the name is threatened by the duplication of the name *Laureta* into *Laurea* (ll. 9, 12). In a way, the sonnet is about the process of duplication. The vision of the real Laura doubles the poet's virtue (l. 6), and the writing of the poem repeats the words of the inner dictator. In these two cases, the doubling is meant to assert the correspondence between language and reality. But as the name Laura is duplicated in "Laurea," the duplication endangers the unity of the proper name and subverts the possibility that the voice of love is bound to an univocal stable sign. The allusion to Apollo in the final tercet, while it draws attention to the poetic act, discloses the symbolic reciprocity—long acknowledged—of "Laura" and "lauro." This Petrarchan conceit (which is multiplied in other variants such as "l'aura," "auro," etc.) shows that desire is always cloaked under false names, that each name is a mask for the restless instability of desire.

Petrarch's idolatry, his so-called narcissism, the palinodic poems—all are willed attempts to fix the endless migrations of desire in a stable form. The impulse for totality and unity is involuntarily blurred by the awareness of the nature of language and desire. Language *betrays* desire, both in the sense that it reveals desire, is its spy, and because language bears an essential otherness to the desire that generates it. At the same time, in the universe of desire totality is never possible: desire knows only shreds and fragments, even if plenitude is its ever elusive mirage. The *Canzoniere* is, to be sure, the attempt to restore the pieces, to give an illusory unity to the fragments. The three hundred and sixty-six poems (the days of the year plus one) simulate the eternal calendar of love, a symbolic order imposed on the fragmentation of time, but the fragments remain as such, "rime sparse." The point is that the unity of the work is the unity *of* fragments and *in* fragments. Not even each fragment, each individual poem, may be said to possess a unity: each poem attempts to begin anew, to be an autonomous and self-enclosed totality, but it inevitably ends up repeating what has already been tried before and leads to other contiguous poems. The poetic sequence is governed by recurrent motifs, such as the phoenix, the sun, the cycle of seasons, metamorphoses, and the like. These motifs, which are in turn metaphors of recurrence constantly alluding to their own instability, disclose the principle of repetition which is at work in the

Canzoniere. Through them, the totality and unity of the text are given as a movement of forms which are discontinuous, which repeat themselves, and fall upon themselves.

It is the metaphor of the labyrinth (explicitly recalled in Sonnets 211 and 224) that best describes the *Canzoniere*: it designates a monadic structure in which the parts are a series of communicating vessels simultaneously proximate and disjointed and in which each partition leads to and separates from another. The metaphor is particularly apt because it also suggests the poet's experience of being locked in a cosmos of his own creation from which there are no exits (as Sonnet 139 dramatizes) and where the only thing left for the poet is to call and make his voice resonate.

Petrarch, as we well know, gives a deliberately melocentric structure to his poetry: the very first sonnet opens with the famous appeal "Voi ch'ascoltate in rime sparse il suono, [You who hear in scattered rhymes the sound]." The sound would seem to constitute, in the poet's general experience of negativity, the irreducible residue of his presence, the domain where the poet's selfhood takes shelter. But the melocentrism of the first sonnet is ironic both because it obscures the moral meaning of the palinode and, more fundamentally, because the sound is hollow, an empty sign which points to its own insubstantiality. In a real sense, the paradigms of the poet's voice are Echo and Orpheus: Echo, the maiden who loves Narcissus and whose love is not returned, is damned to repeat sounds and exist as pure voice, while her body by the mercy of the gods is changed to stone. Orpheus, the poet who wishes to seduce death and recover Eurydice by his song, loses Eurydice. Their voices, like Petrarch's, speak their losses and are veritable allegories of a presence which the self, caught in the riddle of language, can never recover.

MARGUERITE WALLER

Negative Stylistics:
A Reading of the Trionfi

If Canzone 23 identifies a moment or situation in which narrative becomes extremely problematic as a poetic possibility, the *Trionfi*, I would
argue, takes on the ambitious project of attempting to create a new poetics
of narration. Though a much less successful work than the *Canzoniere*, it
departs even more radically from a figural mode of reading and writing,
being a relatively continuous narrative (though probably written over the
course of more than thirty years of Petrarch's life) in which significance is
not recuperative. It is a poem which actively discourages the attempt to
discern figural or allegorical significance in either its own substance or its
(frequently literary historical) subject matter. In proposing the reading of
the *Trionfi* which follows, then, I intend to round out my discussion of the
poetics of Petrarch's Italian poetry—to further substantiate the claims I
have made [elsewhere] concerning the ways in which Petrarch's concept of
history and his poetics implicate each other, and to extend my argument
that Petrarch intends his (and others') texts to be read relationally rather
than figuratively. I would also suggest how literary history serves the
present in retrieving this "unreadable" text of the past. The *Trionfi* seems
to have backfired in its attempt wholly to subvert certain structures of
interpretation, not unlike several more recent texts which, it now appears,
have also stimulated the very readings which their rhetoric most deeply
challenges. Reading the *Trionfi* allegorically or figuratively, as most commentators have done, is like searching for "plot" and "character" in
Finnegans Wake, like trying to determine the "authenticity" of Rousseau's

From *Petrarch's Poetics and Literary History*. © 1980 by the University of Massachusetts Press.

Confessions. In coming to terms with a text which has been misread so thoroughly and which is now mostly unread (though for several centuries the *Trionfi* was more popular than either the *Commedia* or the *Canzoniere*, it now has little appeal, and is usually regarded as "bad" poetry), it becomes necessary to acknowledge two sets of conceptual boundaries, those against which Petrarch's poetry sets itself and those which separate the sensibilities of one time from those of another. The effort to see and understand what Petrarch is doing in the *Trionfi*, therefore, might serve to reintroduce history into our contemporary discussions of "meaning." It would appear at once that present-day theories of discourse are not alone in trying to disassociate meaning from notions of representation, identity, truth, and unity; and that trying to make this break has not always "meant" the same thing.

Our sense of how the *Trionfi* was received in the fifteenth and sixteenth centuries comes from two major sources, notable for their parallel development: written commentaries and pictorial representations. From 1475, when the first extant and universally influential commentary of the poem appeared, until at least 1582, the literary world seems readily to have accepted the *Trionfi* as a moralizing, allegorical representation of the growth and progress of the soul of Everyman as exemplified by the speaker in the poem who was, in turn, taken to be Petrarch. The seminal allegorical gloss of Bernardo da Pietro Lapini da Montalcino, known as Illicino, was echoed by virtually every other Italian commentator for a century and paraphrased as well by Spanish, Portuguese, and German translators. In his 1582 edition with commentary of Petrarch's Italian poetry, Castelvetro presented a fresh and somewhat closer reading of the poem, but he still identified the *Trionfi* thematically as an account of the poet's repentance and conversion. At the close of the century, on the other hand, at the height of the theoretical debate over the epic genre, it seemed to the theoretician Tomaso Costa that the *Trionfi*'s diction, rhetoric, metaphors—"Quella purità e proprietà di lingua, quell' armonia, quella gravità"—were evidence that the work was intended to be an epic.

Pictorial representations of the *Trionfi*, which number in the thousands, evolved along a similar course. Fifteenth- and sixteenth-century pictorial triumphs depict symmetrical series of allegorical figures, seated on chariots drawn by symbolically appropriate beasts, surrounded by groups of captives and attendants. As artists as well as writers of the sixteenth century were drawn to the heroic, the triumphal motif becomes more classically drawn, the groups of captives and attendants more heroically full of literary and historical characters. But with these stylistic changes, the series becomes more rather than less continuous and unified. The iconography of these paintings, frescoes, medals, miniatures, birth trays, *cassoni* or chests, and tapestries is at once so standardized and so discrepant from the poem itself that the puzzle of Renaissance illustrations of the *Trionfi* has become a major art historical preoccupation. Since the earliest paintings predate Illicino, art historians have thought that perhaps an allegorizing commentary, now lost, was written between the first appearance of the poem and its first pictorial representation. This hypothesis, of course, merely begs our question. Whichever came first, an allegorizing written commentary, or an allegorizing painted commentary, the fact remains that both commentators and artists, and presumably their publics, appear to have responded to the poem as if it presented a model of allegorical and visionary coherence. Indeed, the device or motif of the triumph, first made available by Petrarch, remained enormously popular as a vehicle for the presentation of ideas and ideals for three centuries after he wrote.

The *Trionfi* itself, I would maintain, is a radically anti-allegorical, nonvisionary poem; the triumph motif, as Petrarch uses it, is a literary construct chosen to call attention to the fictive nature of both the dream vision and the dreamer who dreams it. The two most obvious sources of the motif already suggest as much. The *Commedia* is once again close to the surface of Petrarch's writing, a relationship underscored in the *Trionfi* by its appropriation of *terza rima* as well as by its all-pervasive verbal and thematic echoes of Dante's poem. The work bears a specific resemblance to the pageant of Beatrice and the Church Militant in the last four cantos of *Purgatorio*. Significantly, Dante's elaborate, highly stylized triumph calls attention to itself as spectacle *as opposed to* event. It represents a departure from the narrative mode in which it is embedded, substituting artifice for event, presumably because at this point the distinction between letter and spirit, between the literal and the figural, begins to break down. It serves as a bridge to the poetics of *Paradiso* where Dante largely abandons narrative, where the "literal" reality with which the pilgrim is confronted remains by definition out of reach of mortal minds, where all the poetry is "equally" metaphorical. A brief evocation by John Freccero of the poetics of *Paradiso* is relevant by contrast, to the direction taken by Petrarch in the *Trionfi:* "It is in difference that meaning is born, like the difference between two phonetic sounds, unintelligible in themselves, yet constituting meaning when linked together. So with the poem, which manages to approach its conclusion and silence by the gradual dissipation of all difference between light and light, and yet remains as the shadow of all that the experience is not, as irreducibly literary as 'a pearl upon a milk white brow.' " Petrarch, in adopting the atypical mode of the Dantesque triumph for his *entire* poem, seems to indicate that even ordinary events, images, and realities are somehow "out of reach." History is indecipherable, and the beautiful fictions of poets remain the only source of pattern and coherence, though they are no longer allegories of anything but themselves. Difference, as we shall see shortly, is irreducibly literary in the *Trionfi*, but gradually exaggerated, not dissipated. The meanings which would be born of different elements rhetorically associated by such means as spatial contiguity, synecdochal representation, exemplification, etc., become unintelligible as the poem renounces the rhetorical means by which such linkages are made, and approaches its own particular version of completion and silence.

The other clearly recognizable model of the Petrarchan motif is the Roman military triumph, descriptions of which Petrarch had read in Roman histories as well as in medieval compilations. But, as Petrarch's countless remarks in letters, meditations, other poems, and the *Trionfi* itself indicate, he conceived of the Roman civilization whose glory was embodied in the triumph as definitively past, as absent from the present. As I noted in my opening chapter, he warned that Rome was an empty name; the reality to which it once pointed, though superior to his own degenerate society, was lost. "Non far idolo un nome / Vano senza soggetto." In the *Trionfi* the speaker portrays himself as deeply enamored of idols, images, and empty names, but none of them, finally, takes precedence over another. Instead they work against each other or cancel each other out, depriving their succession of metaphorical or paradigmatic coherence. No total picture or global view of life ever emerges, while the fluidity and instability of the categories in terms of which such views might be constructed are insisted upon.

The *Trionfi*'s own characteristic narrative strategy is all the more conspicuous for its avoidance of any transcendent design, once the fictive status of the poem's thematic contents has been suggested. The attraction that a succession of apparently autonomous, if radically fictive, performances holds for the poem's protagonist gives the poem its chief means of forwarding the plot, such as there is a plot. At the beginning of the poem, for example, the speaker recounts how, when he sank into sleep in a *chiuso loco* or enclosed place, on an anniversary of his first falling in love, a burst of light ushered in a scene of pomp and circumstance which transported him not only out of his own state of mind, but out of the lackluster reality of his century. The vision of a great lord, "com' un di

color che 'n Campidoglio / trionfal carro a gran gloria conduce (like one
of those which the triumphal chariot bore to great glory on the Capital"
["Triumphus cupidinis" 1.14–15]), promises a new field of vision, perhaps
even an alternative to an intractable reality:

> I' che gioir di tal vista non soglio
> per lo secol noioso in ch' i' mi trovo,
> voto d' ogni valor, pien d' ogni orgoglio,
>   l' abito in vista sì leggiadro e novo
> mirai, alzando gli occhi gravi e stanchi
> ch'altro diletto che 'mparar non provo.

(Unused to rejoicing in such a sight, because of the tiresome
century in which I live, devoid of valor, full of pride, I looked
upon this delightful, astonishing sight, and, raising my tired
and heavy eyes, I feel no other inclination than to learn about
it.)

("Triumphus cupidinis" 1.16–21)

This is only the first of many occasions upon which the poet is
completely removed out of one scene into another without displaying any
capacity or inclination to integrate them conceptually. On another occasion the dramatic possibilities of conflict and tension not only go undevel-
oped, but are actively dissolved and dispersed by the poem's refusal to
remain within any one framework long enough for these tensions to build.
After Massinissa, a figure encountered in the second *capitolo* of the
"Triumphus cupidinis," finishes recounting the story of the conflict between his love for the Carthaginian queen Sophonisba and his duty to the
Roman Empire, a story which Petrarch had told elsewhere, in his Latin epic
the *Africa*, and which here causes the poet-dreamer to dissolve in pity,
Sophonisba herself abruptly enters the conversation to announce that she
still does not like Italians. Much to the amusement of Massinissa, she and
the poet-dreamer thereupon begin arguing about politics, and the melan-
choly mood is broken. Sophonisba has the last word: *s'Africa pianse,
Italia non ne rise: / demandatene pur l' istorie vostre* (if Africa weeps, Italy
does not smile on account of it: just look in your own histories ["Triumphus
cupidinis" 2.83–84]), and Massinissa smiles at the point scored against
his own homeland. History, suddenly, stretches out beyond the end of the
story of Sophonisba's death which becomes only a minor incident in a
temporary reversal.

Such freedom, the fluidity of history's shape, the ease with which political and personal lines are drawn and redrawn, can be exhilarating, but it can also begin to look like too much of a good thing. The most striking example of the poem's antidramatics is the reapparance of Laura, declaring her complete reciprocation of the poet's feeling for her, in a dream he has after witnessing her death in the "Triumphus mortis." Once again the poetic effect is achieved by getting beyond endings, the most definitive of which would seem to be death. Laura rises up from beyond the veil of misapprehensions, dreads, and fears which oppress the "living" to dispel the errors of her deluded lover:

> "Viva son io e tu se' morto ancora,"
> diss' ella, "e sarai sempre infin che giunga
> per levarti di terra l' ultima ora."

("I am alive and you are still dead," she said, "and so you will be until the final hour arrives to lift you from the earth.")

("Triumphus mortis" 2.22–24)

His greatest misapprehension has been, of course, that she did not love him. In creating this impression, he is told, she has been a benevolent and successful manipulator of appearances. She explains:

> Mai diviso
> da te non fu 'l mio cor, né già mai fia;
> ma temprai la tua fiamma col mio viso.

(Never has my heart been divided from you, nor will it ever be; but I tempered your flame with my face.)

("Triumphus mortis" 2.88–90)

Now, it seems, her past behavior can finally be demystified:

> Questi fur teco miei ingegni e mie arti:
> or benigne accoglienze ed ora sdegni;
> tu 'l sai che n' ai cantato in molte parti.

(These were my arts and strategems with you: now gentle welcome and now disdain; you know this who have sung of it in many places.)

("Triumphus mortis" 2.109–11)

This explanation or new interpretation of Laura's gestures and expressions while on earth, though, is as suspect as the easy pieties with which the dream-Laura opens the exchange. What proof is there that this dream within a dream has any substance to it, that it is not simply the product of the dreamer's own distressed imagination? In an odd turn, the poet-dreamer tearfully confesses his own difficulty in believing her and her words, despite his desire to do so. His doubt elicits sixteen *terzine* of attempts on the part of the phantom Laura to prove, by recalling and analyzing various of their past encounters, that she means what she says, that this vision is trustworthy. We may feel that she protests too much, but her lover's response is somewhat different. However questionable or fleeting his moment of retrospective illumination may be, the imposition of "meaning" or "meaningfulness" on what had previously been at best an ambiguous situation succeeds in soothing and relieving him:

> "Quant'io soffersi mai, soave e leve,"
> dissi, "m' ha fatto il parlar dolce e pio."

("However much I have ever suffered," I said, "your sweet and pious words have made me calm and happy.")

("Triumphus mortis" 2.184–85)

The opposite conclusion remains to be inferred from the way this episode is *written*. We have just learned, the storyteller herself has just explained, how easily the arts of expression can be manipulated and used to manipulate. We then observe the poet-dreamer succumb to precisely this sort of manipulation. Neither his response nor the ambiguous status of the dream-within-a-dream establishes the authority of the phantom Laura's version of the relationship over the earlier version enacted in the Triumphs of Love and Chastity. Rather than a vertical hierarchy of interpretations approaching closer and closer to the truth, we find a horizontal succession of situations operating such that whatever is most immediate seems most authoritative, or at least most compelling, to the dreamer. Petrarch's wording and the positioning of his words are very careful here—"Quant'io soffersi mai, soave e leve," / dissi, "m' ha fatto il parlar dolce e pio." The present, *soave e leve*, does not retrospectively reinterpret the past, *Quant'io soffersi mai*, but opposes and supplants it.

Undermining even the horizontal succession of meanings and attracting critical attention more specifically to the interpretive or perceptual habits of the dreamer himself, there are a whole range of such non sequiturs which serve throughout the poem to intensify the kinds of interpretive conflict which the larger movements somewhat crudely and ostentatiously appease. Though each of the six triumphs—in order the "Triumphus cupidinis," the "Triumphus pudicitie," the "Triumphus mortis," the "Triumphus fame," the "Triumphus temporis," and the "Triumphus eternitatis"—appears to the dreamer to present an alternative to the view or vision that precedes it (even the initial "Triumphius cupidinis," it should be noted), it is especially these oppositions that prove spurious as soon as they are examined closely. The splendid procession at the opening of the "Triumphus cupidinis," for example, manages at once to cast a great light (*una gran luce* [1.11]) which dazzles, and a gloomy pall (*l'aer fosco* [1.46]) which obstructs, the dreamer's vision. (One quickly understands why illustrators, in particular, ignored Petrarch's text when trying to visualize this apparition.) It has caused the dreamer to rejoice, yet it is filled with a dreariness which pointedly recalls his mood just prior to falling asleep:

> Ivi fra l'erbe, già del pianger fioco,
> vinto dal sonno, vidi una gran luce
> e dentro assai dolor con breve gioco.

(There, on the grass, already weak from weeping, overcome by sleep, I saw a great light and within much grief and little joy.)

("Triumphus cupidinis" 1.10–12)

Once it is established that he will try to apprehend the nature of Love through learning about Love's captives, further problems arise. The figures themselves have, if anything, progressively less in common. At times they are grouped, like the lovers from Ovid's *Heroides*, according to a common literary source. Once the dreamer finds Love represented by two sets of figures who, except for their contiguity and equality in number, are diametrically opposed:

> Vedi tre belle donne innamorate:
> Procri, Artemisia con Deidamia,
> ed altrettante ardite e scelerate:
> Semiramis, Bibli e Mirra ria.

(I saw three beautiful, enamored ladies: Procris, Artemisia, and with them Deidamia, and just as many who were bold and wicked: Semiramis, Byblis, and evil Myrrha).

("Triumphus cupidinis," 3.73–76)

Conversely, the same figure may exemplify, in antithetical ways, two different concepts. Caesar, who goes in chains as a captive in Love's triumph, occupies the position of highest honor, next to the triumphatrix herself, in the "Triumphus fame." This semiotic instability is certainly compounded by, and perhaps partially attributable to, the intellectual and emotional limitations of the perceiver. What he has seen and felt attracted to can be completely incommensurable with what he has been capable of assimilating and narrating:

> Era si pieno il cor di meraviglie
> ch'i stava come l'uom che non po dire,
> e tace, e guarda pur ch'altri 'l consiglie.

(My heart was so full of marvels that I was like a man who cannot speak and falls silent and watches for another to counsel him.)

("Triumphus cupidinis" 3.1–3)

Once the dreamer feels he *does* understand the paradoxes and contradictions of love, his comprehension proves to be the most unreliable indicator of all. Captivated by an apparition of his own beloved, he becomes quite literally a captive, one of the prisoners in Love's train. Temporarily his new "knowledge," as he calls it, liberates him from the past definite of time-bound observations and allows him a thirty-five line interlude in an ahistorical present:

> Or so come da sé 'l cor si disgiunge
> e come sa far pace, guerra e tregua,
> e coprir suo dolor, quand' altri il punge;
>
> . . . .
>
> so come sta tra' fiori ascoso l'angue,
> come sempre tra due si vegghia e dorme,
> come senza languir si more e langue.

(Now I know how the heart is separated from itself and how it knows to make peace, war, and truce, and to hide its grief, when another pierces it. . . . I know how the serpent hides itself among the flowers, how one always sleeps and wakes between two contraries, how without suffering illness, one may die and suffer.)

("Triumphus cupidinis" 3.151–53, 157–59)

Not surprisingly, though, he soon finds himself trapped, not in the past (or not only in the past), but in a particularly confining *tenebrosa e stretta gabbia* ("Triumphus cupidinis" 4.157), a gloomy and cramped cage, where Love's other followers no longer appear a means to knowledge, but become instead mere empty images.

It is important at this point to consider the mechanism of this entrapment as well as its consequences. The remaining five *trionfi* are all called into being in one way or another by the threat it poses. It happens for the first time at the moment when the dreamer is wholly "captivated," when, in other words, he no longer has one eye on the *chiuso loco* and one on the dream landscape, but has had his focus shifted entirely into the dream. What was at first pertinent to him because of its difference from and apparent opposition to his waking state, finally usurps his entire field of vision. His heart has become, as he says he knows, separated from itself—"Or so come da sé 'l cor si disgiunge"—for his "understanding" is more accurately a forgetting of the relational aspect of the antithesis out of which a new sense of self and self-knowledge has been constituted.

It is the illusion of autonomy, of a self which provides the common ground for contraries and conflicts, to which the poem here addresses itself. For Petrarch the associations with this problem are Dantesque. The fatally compelling image of the dreamer's beloved appears just after Dante's Paolo and Francesca have been mentioned, and the dreamer's capitulation is similar to theirs. Dante's lovers, we recall, allowed the fiction of Lancelot and Guinivere to preempt the present moment of their reading of that fiction. By "forgetting" their own role in constituting the text in terms of which they chose to govern themselves, they, in a sense, made fictions of themselves. The structure of the *Commedia*, of course, comments ironically on this mode of self-definition. The couple's historically defined identities reassert themselves, appropriately, in the person of Francesca's husband who is also Paolo's brother. He cuts short their idyll, he and the Infernal context in which we hear this story casting the baselessness of the lovers' readings of themselves and of each other into relief.

The crucial difference between Paolo and Francesca and Petrarch's dreamer is that the latter's act of misreading seems to have been unavoidable. He has not "chosen." As in the story of Paolo and Francesca, self-entrapment is not the solution to the indeterminacy of experience, but Petrarch does not oppose, as Dante seems to, the possibility of a historically grounded self-reading to the purely fictive readings within which people imprison themselves. The dreamer's "punishment" is, in fact, emblematic of his situation before *and* after his captivation:

> In così tenebrosa e stretta gabbia
> rinchiusi fummo, ove le penne usate
> mutai per tempo e la mia prima labbia;
>   e'ntanto, pur sognando libertate,
> l'alma, che 'l gran desio fea pronta e leve,
> consolai col veder le cose andate.

Rimirando er'io fatto al sol di neve
tanti spirti e sì chiari in carcer tetro,
quasi lunga pittura in tempo breve,
    che 'l piè va innanzi e l'occhio torna a dietro.

(In such a gloomy and cramped cage I was enclosed where in
the course of time I changed my accustomed feathers and my
first face, while, only dreaming of liberty, I consoled my spirit,
which my great desire made impressionable and eager, with the
sight of by-gone things. I became like snow in the sun, gazing at
so many illustrious souls in the gloomy prison, like a long
picture seen in a short time, such that the foot goes forward
and the eye turns back.)

("Triumphus cupidinis" 4.157–67)

Ever since Orpheus, the eye turning to look behind as the dreamer's does
has been emblematic of a kind of nostalgic reification which falsifies the
power of a metaphor to shape and to motivate action. But here the
dreamer is faced with a situation in which *any* interpretive position yields
a reification. Though he does not deny time or history, whose passage
manifests itself in the signs of aging he notes, this "historical" self is itself
an ambiguous entity. *L'usate penne* and *la prima mia labbia* do not, at any
rate, distinguish between the covering of his head and his writing imple-
ments, between facial features and the organ which forms speech out of
sound. As has been indicated, analogously, by his disinclination or inabil-
ity to locate his story definitely in either the past tense of "event" or the
present tense of narration (the poem slips back and forth between the two
almost from the very beginning), the narrator or dreamer himself, at any
and all points in the text, is hardly less "fictive" than any part of his
dream. Perhaps during such historical times, in a century described as
"voto d'ogni valor, pien d'ogni orgoglio (devoid of any value, full of every
pretension" ["Triumphus cupidinis" 1.18]), an "historically grounded self-
reading" is necessarily indistinguishable from self-delusion; the "ground"
in terms of which this "self" is constituted is, in any case, the first cause of,
rather than the solution to, the problem of self-positioning. Compounding
the problem such a self becomes all the more vulnerable to the kind of
stabilized and stabilizing illusion represented by the dreamer's pseudo-
revelation. The dreamer's *libertate*, not excepting the liberation from his
own *secol noioso* apparently effected by the initial stages of Love's triumph,
has been a dream all along.

The absence of historical grounding is, in other words, a hermeneutic problem in the *Trionfi*, and not the *prima radice* of sin which the denial of historicity becomes in the *Commedia*. This problem is taken up again in all the succeeding trionfi, but the fifth trionfo, the "Triumphus temporis," is perhaps the most immediately relevant. There the dreamer discovers that the kinds of order—political, intellectual, or artistic—that are made of experience are only as real as the infrastructure on which they depend, and that neither human authors nor that which they presume to authorize remain constant. The sun, the titular figure of the trionfo, saves his special ire for those who think to escape the common lot through their relatively durable political or poetic codifications of significance:

> Vidi una gente andarsen queta queta
> senza temer di Tempo o di sua rabbia,
> che gli avea in guardia istorico o poeta.
>   Di lor par che più d'altri invidia s'abbia,
> che per se stessi son levati a volo
> uscendo for della commune gabbia.

(I saw a people going very quietly without fear of Time or of his wrath, because poets and historians were standing guard. Of these it appeared that the sun was most envious, since, escaping from the common cage, they had risen in flight through their own efforts.)

("Triumphus temporis," ll. 88–93)

Once again, the escape is illusory. The more absolute or immutable or beautiful the construct seems, the more it falsifies and deceives. The dreamer hears a voice saying:

> Passan vostre grandezze e vostre pompe,
> passan le signorie, passano i regni:
> ogni cosa mortal Tempo interrompe,
>   e ritolta a' men buon, non dà a' più degni;
> e non pur quel di fuori il Tempo solve,
> ma le vostre eloquenzie e' vostri ingegni.
>
> . . . .
>
>   Or perché umana gloria à tante corna,
> non é mirabil cosa, s'a fiaccarle
> alquanto oltra l'usanza si soggiorna.

(Your grandeur and displays pass away, your rulerships pass and your kingdoms: Time interrupts every mortal thing, and

what it has retaken from the less good, it does not give to the
more worthy; and Time does not dissolve only external things,
but your eloquence and your genius . . . only because human
glory has so many branches it is not surprising if to exhaust
them all sometimes takes longer than usual.)

                    ("Triumphus temporis," ll. 112–17, 121–23)

As in the "Triumphus cupidinis," the satisfaction of definition, the illusion
of understanding, offer a baseless seduction. The better, the more complex
and comprehensive the metaphor, the greater the lie. It is not just that
these intellectual and spiritual accomplishments are perishable; they are
useless, or worse yet, self-defeating, as ways of apprehending and adapting
to a world in which the central fact is the absence of any ontological
structure of the sort implied by the "understandings" they present. The
voice heard by the dreamer is itself subject to a significant error. The
"interruption" or breaking off of mortal things attributed to Time, itself an
intellectual/linguistic construct, harks back to the rupture or discontinuity
which takes place between the uncertainty of relational perception and the
achievement of a unifying interpretive position. Time may be a way of
measuring the extent of this rupture in historical terms, but its apparent
power, too, is a function of convention—*l'usanza*. Time does not prove the
lie of metaphor; it is a metaphor whose own discontinuity proves the lie of
Time's would-be distinction between presence and its passing (Passan
vostre grandezze e vostre pompe, / passan *le signorie*, passano *i regni*), and
demonstrates the equivalence (captured in the ambiguity of the Italian *il
Tempo* solve) of resolution and dissolution.

　　It is worth considering, at this point, the criticisms made of the poem
by those critics who have maintained that Petrarch (in the fourteenth
century) would have written this way only if he lacked the talent to do
otherwise. What modern Petrarch scholars look for and fail to find in the
Trionfi is an overarching design which would serve as a corrective for the
narrator's limited and confusing phenomenological perspective, which would
serve at least to distinguish Petrarch from the dreamer and the dreamer
from the dream. Thomas Bergin, an astute reader of Petrarch, explains:
"The basic flaw derives from a constitutional incapacity of Petrarch to
handle the grand design. . . . Even on such a simple level as the narrative
plane, his work lacks consistency; the central figure is partly narrator,
partly actor, partly a man with a vision, partly commentator." This is
indeed the ambiguous position of the dreamer, and Bergin does a good job
characterizing it. What he does not see is that this position is consistent

with the other poetic strategies of the *Trionfi* and with its conceptual problematic. To distinguish a reliable narrator and a clear-cut narrative object would be to counteract all that the poem tries to accomplish. Were Petrarch to do so, he could indeed be accused of incompetence. Just as useful (and just as perfectly mistaken) is Umberto Bosco's criticism of Petrarch's descriptive power in the characterization of personnel and physical surroundings in the *Trionfi*. A battle scene between Amor and Laura, the titular figure in the "Triumphus pudicitie," is but murkily rendered. We are given no description of the terrain, and Laura herself is described by a series of negative comparisons:

> Non fan sì grande e sì terribil sono
>
> Non corse mai sì levemente al varco
>
> che giàmmai schermidor non fu sì accorto
> a schifar colpo, nè nocchier sì presto
> a volger nave dagli scogli in porto
>
> Non ebbe mai di vero valor dramma Camilla
>
> non fu sì ardente Cesare in Farsaglia
>
> Non fu 'l cader di subito sì strano
> dopo tante vittorie ad Anniballe,
>
> non freme così 'l mar quando s'adira,
> non Inarime allor che Tifeo piange,
> Né Mongibel s'Encelado sospira.

(Never make so great and terrible a sound

Never ran so swiftly to the pass

Never was there a fencer so adept at dodging blows
nor pilot so ready to turn the ship from the reefs
in port.

Camilla's valor was no more than a dram

Caesar was not as ardent in Pharsalia

The sudden fall of Hannibal was not so strange

The sea does not rage thus when it is angry, nor Ischia
when Typhoeus weeps, nor Etna when Enceladus sighs.)
                         (ll. 25, 37, 49–51, 70–71, 73, 97–98, 112–14)

By the end of the battle, Laura has been compared in this way to a lion, a thunderbolt, a flame, a whirlwind, a deer fleeing a leopard, a fencer dodging blows, a pilot who skillfully avoids reefs, Camilla the amazon, Caesar, Scipio, David, and Judith. Laura's characteristic gestures of aggressively avoiding, dodging, or consuming material objects and obstacles is missed by Bosco, all of whose sensibilities are outraged: "I leave aside the comparisons with which Love, her adversary, is blessed. All this to say simply that Love bends his bow against Laura." Bosco ends by dismissing this excessive use of negatives as a floundering of the poet's imagination. That he can formulate no clear picture of the scene and its action from this kind of description, however, is one measure of its success as a stylistic *tour de force* in the poem's own terms. The negative comparisons, especially, represent an elegant refinement of the poem's general principle. No less than would positive comparisons, they evoke images and associations, but the reader is simultaneously told he must put them aside. The mind carries away impressions and attitudes, but is not allowed to stop and dwell upon any of them. The incompatibility of the similes with each other, except as they doubly avoid the object, works toward the same end. It protects Chastity's triumph against the kind of imaginative assent that would be invited by more stable metaphors. What both Bergin and Bosco at once see and do not see in the poem is its concerted experimentation in *negative stylistics*, a subversion of the delicate yet tyrannical operations of a more usual, but here inadequate, aesthetic sensibility.

Chastity herself, in fact, comes to represent resistance to the coercion of style offered by more positive formulations, as well as to the seduction of self-evident "truths" which an elegantly polished, authoritative text might have to offer. Her defeat of Amor in the second trionfo is followed in the so-called "Triumphus mortis" by a startling scene in which she takes issue with the eloquent threats of the imposing black-robed figure of Death, and it is Death who backs down. The poem makes its point dramatically rather than didactically (to be didactic would be to fall into one of the very modes it subverts) by portraying their exchange in direct discourse. Death announces herself:

> O tu, donna, che vai
> di gioventute e di bellezze altera,
> e di tua vita il termine non sai,
>   io son colei che sì importuna e fera
> chiamata son da voi, e sorda e cieca
> gente, a cui si fa notte innanzi sera;
>
> .   .   .   .

> Or a voi, quando il viver più diletta,
> drizzo 'l mio corso innanzi che Fortuna
> nel vostro dolce qualche amaro metta.

(Oh you, lady, who go proud of your youth and beauty, and do
not know when your life will end, I am she who is called
relentless and fierce by you and by people blind and deaf, for
whom night comes before evening. . . . Now to you, when life
is most delightful, I direct my course before Fortune adds any
bitterness to your pleasure.)

("Triumphus mortis" 1.34–39, 46–48)

But Laura, the embodiment of rhetorical as well as physical chastity,
refuses to accept this formulation, especially as it imperiously defines
herself and her companions:

> In costor non ài tu ragione alcuna
> ed in me poca: solo in questa spoglia.
>
> .   .   .   .
>
> Altri so che n'avrà più di me doglia,
> la cui salute dal mio viver pende;
> a me fia grazia che di qui me scioglia.

(Over these with me you have no right and you have very little
over me; only over my bodily garment. I know another who
will grieve more than I, whose well-being depends upon my
life; to me it were a blessing to be released from here.)

("Triumphus mortis" 1.49–50, 52–54)

Death, whose discourse was intended to subordinate the partial view of
her victims to her own more comprehensive view, has the rug pulled out
from under her by Laura's untroubled willingness to shed such earthly
"garments" altogether. As Laura has further pointed out, Death can signify only to the living, and it is the living who variously decide its
significance. Death stands corrected:

> Qual è chi 'n cosa nova gli occhi intende
> e vede ond'al principio non s'accorse,
> di ch'or si meraviglia e si riprende,
> tal si fe' quella fera.

(As one who bends her eyes on something new and sees what at

first she had not noticed, at which she marvels and corrects
herself, such was that fierce creature.)

("Triumphus mortis" 1.55–58)

Laura's compassionate aside concerning the benighted poet who will take
Death at her word is perhaps Petrarch's ironic comment upon the writer's
particular vulnerability to the power of authoritative discourse. It is notable that Death is by far the more overtly "poetic" figure of the two, and
that she behaves as if she could not properly *see* the less rhetorically
pretentious Laura.

This poetry, though, is as aggressively and promiscuously chaste as
Chastity/Laura herself. It is utterly innocent, for example, of structurally
significant geographical or cosmological landmarks. The effortless translo-
cations of the spectacle from a closed valley to Amor's palace/prison on
Cyprus and to Chastity's temple in Rome via Scipio's solitary retreat at
Literno are the opposite of the arduous step-by-step Dantesque account of
descent and ascent. Petrarch's foreign scenes have a studio air about them.
They are the same set with different names. Or as Bosco puts it, "if
sometimes he describes, and it happens very rarely, it is always the landscape of Vaucluse" (the site of Petrarch's most permanent home, and the
setting of many of his poems). The numerous figures whom the dreamer
encounters all share the same ground, or better, they share a kind of
groundlessness. They occupy no particular place in the physical or moral
universe. Similarly, the poem's donnée, that the spectator remains station-
ary relative to the transitory spectacle, suggests that Petrarch does not aspire
to transcend the individual, subjective perspective. This conspicuous reversal of the Dantesque situation signals Petrarch's profound estrangement
from the poetics of transcendence.

Very pointedly in the "Triumphus eternitatis," where one might expect some panoramic cosmological ratification of the pilgrim's progress,
the "vision" becomes instead completely interior:

> Questo pensava, e mentre più s'interna
> la mente mia, veder mi parve un mondo
> novo, in etate immobile ed eterna.

(This I was thinking, and while my mind goes into itself more
deeply, I seem to see a new world, in an immobile and eternal
state.)

("Triumphus eternitatis," ll. 19–21)

The version of eternity which follows has more to do with the changes that the absence of "time" would make in the mental processes of perception and intellection than it does with what the mind might then perceive and understand. The poet locates his paradise grammatically and syntactically rather than cosmologically:

> Quel che l'anima nostra preme e 'ngombra:
> "dianzi, adesso, ier, diman, mattino e sera"
> tutti in un punto passeran com' ombra;
>   non avrà loco "fu" "sarà" né "era,"
> ma "è" solo, "in presente," ed "ora" ed "oggi"
> e sola "eternità" raccolta e 'ntera.

(That which oppresses and encumbers us: "previously, now, yesterday, tomorrow, morning, evening," all these will pass like a shadow into one point; "was," "will be" and "used to be" will have no place, but only "is," "in the present" and "now" and "today" and only "eternity" gathered together and entire.)

("Triumphus eternitatis," ll. 64–69)

In discussing the "Triumphus temporis" I noted that the voice heard by the dreamer was mistaken in attributing the insubstantialization of mortal things to time. The solution offered by Time to the problem of metaphor—everything passes away—denied the terms of the problem. The error recurs here, in the final trionfo, but in a significantly different form. Time, which I described earlier as "an intellectual/linguistic construct," is explicitly characterized now as an assemblage of grammatical and syntactic elements—adverbs, verb tenses, temporal nouns—which distinguish states of mind and carry the weight of senses of time. In other words, the rupture between the unstable perception of a persona and a unitary position, which was first analyzed apropos of the "Triumphus cupidinis" in rhetorical terms, is finally recast here as a grammatical problem. The "oppression" and "encumbrance" of uncertain relational moments is that of verb tenses, adverbs, and temporal nouns; and the "paradise" of a unified position which is aspired to is a language of presence, a language, that is, of the present tense ("is," "now," etc.). But, though the error need no longer be understood as one of rhetorical construction, the verbal sleight of hand that would grammatically heal the rupture is no less problematic. To arrive at—that is, to describe—this "place" or "position" is not to represent it, to present objects or a landscape, but to present a linguistic possibility, and yet the terms of this verbal presentation of a utopian language are the very terms which such a language would deny. The future tense "will have no place," the past tense "will [be] . . . *gathered*," and the sense of "gathered together entire" are non-sense without a sense of syntactic fragmentation and dispersal. The language which has "no place" for the temporality of grammar and syntax is, in fact, a "no place" (*u-topos*) in terms of that grammar and syntax.

It is specifically the ground for figural interpretation that Petrarch definitively dissolves by means of this final restatement of the problem, and he pointedly refers here to those, not unlike his persona in Canzone 23, who persist in trying to play the figural "game":

> Quasi spianati dietro e 'nnanzi i poggi
> ch'occupavan la vista, non fia in cui
> vostro sperare e rimembrar s'appoggi;
>   la qual varietà fa spesso altrui
> vaneggiar sì che 'l viver pare un gioco,
> pensando pur: "che sarò io? che fui?"

(The hills having been flattened before and behind which used to occupy the view, there will not be that on which your hope and remembrance might lean; whose variation often makes people rave so that to live appears a game, so that they think only: "What shall I be? What have I been?")

("Triumphus eternitatis," ll. 70–75)

The game referred to here is the play of difference (*varietà*) between two temporal positions which have just been shown to be equally insubstantial. The future is as much an optical illusion as the past. The subject and its present represent a compound version of this error. In order to define itself, to "mean" something, the subject at once constitutes and is constituted by a reification of the arbitrary syntactical relationship between these two positions.

Nonetheless, Petrarch, no more than Dante, attributes this "false" figural reification to the tradition of Christian figural interpretation. Petrarch's poetics discourages figural modes of thought and interpretation, not, I would infer, to foster secular nihilism, but to undercut the secular "reality" that Petrarch claims to find in de facto dominance in the world around him. The dream vision, we recall, is not finally separable from the unprepossessing historical situation out of which it arises; the uncertain perspective offered by this situation must itself be understood to be as partial and contingent as the perspective that might be achieved at any other moment. I would further support my inference by making some concluding observations about the feature of the poem which has proved the greatest stumbling block of all to modern readers.

More than half the poem is taken up with what are often remembered as heavy, monotonous catalogues. These catalogues occur in only three of the six trionfi—the "Triumphus cupidinis," the "Triumphus pudicitie," and the "Triumphus fame"—but they are often thought of as making up the entire work, and they apparently account for much of the literary historical confusion surrounding it. Readers like C. S. Lewis, who determines that "the whole plan of Petrarch's *Trionfi* seems to be devised for the purpose of admitting as many catalogues as possible," assume that Petrarch is ineptly using a rhetorical device commonly found in medieval literature. Lewis suggests that medieval authors (among whom he includes Petrarch) presented encyclopedic information which most of their audience must already have known, and that they did so because author and audience alike found it aesthetically satisfying to dwell on the great imagined structure of their universe. "Every particular fact and story became more interesting and more pleasurable if, by being properly fitted in, it carried one's mind back to the Model as a whole." Thus, although the catalogue was often identified in rhetorical terms as a digression or amplification, it might be regarded functionally as a highly economical means of filling in the total picture. The *Commedia*, the most sophisticated of medieval catalogues, is a supreme example of this economy. It is encyclopedic, not by virtue of naming all the constituents of each class, of being quantitatively comprehensive, but by outlining the articulations of a single, internally consistent system which makes intelligible each of its constituent parts. On each Purgatorial terrace, for instance, one example of a virtue from the life of the Virgin, one from pagan history, and one from Christian history are sufficient to describe the nature of that virtue in terms of all of human history. Typically, the hierarchical arrangement of sins and virtues tells us enough about them that the poet is free to offer idiosyncratic exempla which demand more complicated responses than would the obvious or expected. Considering the scope of the poem, the number of what E. R. Curtius has called its "personnel" is surprisingly low. A significant grouping of a few figures in fact tells us far more than a long list could.

The governing trope which Lewis identifies as characteristic of medieval discourse and which Dante uses so brilliantly is, of course, synecdoche, the substitution of the part for the whole, the species for the genus, or the genus for the species. This use of synecdoche depends upon and implies a whole system of hierarchically ordered (though not necessarily reified) relationships. It is a trope of *totalization*. Its prominence in medieval literature suggests, as Lewis says, a conception of the universe as a coherent totality. Conversely, our immunity to the potency of medieval catalogues may reflect both the changes that have occurred in our modes of conceptualization and the loss of the sense of intimacy with the "universe" that these changes have entailed. Nevertheless, as Bergin's complaints about the catalogues in the *Trionfi* make clear, any age would be hard put to do without synecdoches of a less global sort. For Bergin, Petrarch "lacked the discretion (God's gift to Dante) to keep the informational drive under control." In the "Triumphus fame," the enumeration seems endless, and the efforts of the poet to find phrases of individual definition or distinction are painful to observe.

Bergin is quite right to sense that there is something very different about Petrarch's catalogues. Petrarch has gone out of his way, especially in his use of the catalogue, not to imply synecdochally the existence of a hierarchical system, a controlling idea, or a coherent universe. That his catalogues are exhaustive and exhausting, that his narrator must try to name *all* the figures in a given triumph, indicates the absence of any synecdochal understanding that would make this arduous, empirical approach to the whole unnecessary. And despite the length of the catalogues, Petrarch conscientiously avoids giving the impression that they ever succeed in being all-inclusive. In a moment of funny but poignant self-parody at the beginning of the second capitolo of the "Triumphus fame," the poet compares his "vision" of eminent Romans to the "historical" texts on the basis of which their actions and reputations have traditionally been inferred, commenting that between those texts and his narrative there are large discrepancies:

> Giungea la vista con l'antiche carte
> ove son gli alti nomi e' sommi pregi,
> e sentiv'al mio dir mancar gran parte.

> (I compared what I saw with ancient documents where the great names and highest reputations are, and perceived that much was missing from my account.)
>
> ("Triumphus fame" 2.4–6)

This confrontation opens upon an infinite regression of discrepancies. The differences between Petrarch's textual fiction and those texts which are also (or have become) historical ones do not, on the one hand, even begin to approximate the difference or disjunction between those texts and the "realities" they preserve, nor can those "realities" themselves be said to escape the problems of textuality, understood in Petrarchan terms. The *alti nomi* or great *names* and the *sommi pregi* or highest *reputations* which "are" in the *antiche carte* exist at once nowhere else and not there either. On the other hand, we later learn in the "Triumphus temporis" that the "authorities" are incomplete in another way, due to losses incurred over the years. And, in any case, the dreamer is too quickly distracted by the appearance of a group of non-Roman notables, *pellegrini egregi*, for the *antiche carte* to be of much help in supplementing the Roman catalogue whose acknowledged incompleteness initiated this meditation. The dreamer has difficulty not only in naming the members of one species, but also in isolating one species from another. The pain and perplexity experienced by Bergin are his as well.

Nevertheless, the roll call of the illustrious is complete enough that certain figures are conspicuous by their absence, and we discover that the *lacunae* strikingly confirm what the disproportionate length and apparent raggedness of the catalogues imply. Bergin's scholarly wondering about Petrarch's omissions probably approximates the reaction the poem intends to provoke: "Whole catalogues of medieval worthies are excluded. There are no great kings: one might have expected St. Louis at least, or, given our poet's devotion to the house of Sicily, Charles of Anjou; and if philosophers, why not Christian Saints?" Here in ghostly form is the economy, the synecdochal use of names and images, which Bergin misses and which Lewis even more amazingly finds in the catalogues as given. The absence of the architects and defenders of the Christocentric model signals the absence, already sensed in the calculated shapelessness of the poem, of the model itself. The only trace of the Christ event, the only occurrence of the name Christ, is the mention of His empty tomb which the contemporary Christian world has abandoned to the Saracens:

> Gite superbi, o miseri Cristiani,
> consumando l'un l'altro, e non vi caglia
> che 'l sepolcro di Cristo è in man de' cani!

(Continue in your pride, O wretched Christians, consuming one another, and let it not matter to you that the sepulchre of Christ is in the hands of dogs.)

("Triumphus fame" 2.142–44)

Christ is as doubly absent as the human subject which, for Augustine or Dante, could be defined in terms of Him; the absence of any other New

Testament figures—there are only Old Testament characters, mentioned in the "Triumphus cupidinis" and the "Triumphus fame"—effectively brackets that chapter of human history which had traditionally been appealed to in making sense of the rest.

The critical interest in the *Trionfi* as a "medievalizing" and ultimately confessional poem is, therefore, misplaced. The poem's few apparently Christian elements occur in the form of empty pieties which serve merely to obscure (for the poem's personae) the consequences of defining the self and its world in exclusively secular terms. On the other hand, it is not necessarily a "modernist" secular poem either; it would not substitute an understanding of linguistic and rhetorical operations for religious understanding. The misimpression that my reading could possibly convey is that Petrarch, in subverting figural interpretation, is subverting only or chiefly Christian figural interpretation. The "new field of vision," or cultural alternative suggested by the rediscovery and revaluation of classical texts (and evoked most powerfully in the opening trionfo), serves, it might seem, simply to burst the bounds of a unified theological-historiographical system of belief. It is precisely this abuse of the "new learning," though, toward which the poetics of the *Trionfi* is consistently directed. A new poetics of history and therefore of narrative needs to be worked out, not in order to reduce Christian history to a mere chapter in a larger volume of historiographical schemata (the option obliquely presented in the episode of Massinissa and Sophonisba and later indirectly criticized in the dream-within-a-dream of Laura after her death), but rather in order to deconstruct *merely* historical understandings of past and present. The point the *Trionfi* makes, in other words, is that *any* historical understanding is inevitably figural, that a new historical understanding replaces one set of metaphorical possibilities with another. To the extent that this irreducible metaphoricity is not understood, historical "knowledge" becomes at best a deception and at worst the agency of moral, spiritual, and perhaps political paralysis. To claim or to appear to claim completeness for one's reading of the past, and, by extension, for one's reading of oneself, is to enlist history in precisely the causes to which it is least suited: those of endowing the moment of discourse with a privileged status, and of masking (or repressing) the ambiguity of its "meaning."

THOMAS M. GREENE

Petrarch
and the Humanist Hermeneutic

A well-known letter from Petrarch to Giovanni Colonna di San Vito evokes a promenade the two men had made together through the wilderness of ruins then covering most of Rome. As he recalls to his friend the sites they had visited, the poet identifies them not as they appeared to the naked eye but as they prompted his historical imagination: "Each step," he writes, "stirred our tongue and mind (Aderat . . . per singulos passus quod linguam et animum excitaret)." The organization of the long touristic catalogue that ensues bears no relation to the disposition of historic sites in Rome—most of which were lost or so overgrown as to be unrecognizable—but follows rather the course of ancient Roman history: "Hic Evandri regia . . . hic Caci spelunca; hic lupa nutrix (Here was the dwelling of Evander . . . here the cave of Cacus, here the nourishing she-wolf)," and so on through the early kings, the republic, the empire, and the Christian martyrs. Since neither Petrarch nor his friend could identify more than a fraction of the actual scenes where the historical or legendary events were supposed to have been enacted, the letter exhibits the imaginative projection onto a landscape of a historical coherence which that landscape could only begin to suggest. Petrarch essentially *read* an order into the Roman wilderness, intuited a plan beneath the shattered temples and grazing sheep whose overwhelming human drama rendered the surface accidents of the city merely evocative pretexts. Oblivious like all his contemporaries to the atmospheric appeal of ruins in themselves, Petrarch might be said to have divined the subterranean plan of a living city in the way a scholar might

From *The Light in Troy: Imitation and Discovery in Renaissance Poetry.* © 1982 by Yale University. Yale University Press, 1982.

puzzle out conjecturally the precious and nearly obliterated text of a palimpsest whereon a debased modern text had been superimposed.

The pursuit of a deeper historical reality beneath unpromising modern appearances leaves its mark on many of Petrarch's works, and especially on those letters that reflect his touristic curiosity. Thus the young Petrarch describes his pleasure in the city now called Cologne as having stemmed from the fanciful reconstructions it provoked:

> Proximis aliquot diebus a mane ad vesperam civitatem iisdem ducibus circumivi, haud iniucundum exercitium, non tam ob id quod ante oculos erat, quam recordatione nostrorum maiorum, qui tam procul a patria monumenta Romanae virtutis tam illustria reliquissent.

> (During the next few days I wandered about the city from morning to night under the guidance of my friends. It was a very pleasant occupation, not so much because of what I actually saw, as from the recollection of our ancestors, who left such illustrious memorials of Roman virtues so far from the fatherland.)

> (*Familiares* 1.5)

A few years later, during his first visit to Rome, he wrote that he had been actually hesitant to arrive, "metuens ne quod ipse michi animo finxeram, extenuarent oculi et magnis semper nominibus inimica presentia (fearing that the sight of actuality would bring low my high imaginations. Present reality is always hostile to greatness" *Familiares* 2.14). But in this case, he added, the present was greater than he expected. It was greater, of course, precisely because it offered sufficient stimulus for the imagination to win its contest with the diminished present.

A long letter to Philippe de Vitry about the itinerary of Cardinal Gui de Boulogne through Italy evokes this prelate's future visit to Rome in terms of the Christian relics he will find there, each of which preserves intact the memory of a past event. The letter then turns to the pagan past of Rome, which also awaits the traveler, and here Petrarch's prose blends almost inextricably the objects of common sight with the objects of the mind's eye:

> Mirabitur septem colles unius muri ambitu circumclusos, cuntis olim terris ac montibus et pelagis imperantes, et latas vias captivorum agminibus tunc angustas; arcus suspiciet triumphales subactorum quondam regum ac populorum spoliis honustos;

Capitolium ascendet omnium caput arcemque terrarum, ubi
olim cella Iovis fuerat, nunc est Ara Coeli, unde, ut memorant,
Augusto Cesari puer Cristus ostensus est.

(He will gaze in wonder at the seven hills enclosed within a
single wall, once supreme over all lands, seas, and mountains;
and the broad streets, all too narrow for the hordes of captives.
He will look up at the triumphal arches, once loaded with the
spoils of subjugated kings and peoples. He will ascend the
Capitoline hill, the world's head, the citadel of all the lands,
where aforetime was Jove's seat, where now stands the *Ara
Coeli*. There, they say, the infant Christ was displayed to Caesar Augustus.)

(Familiares 9.13)

In each instance the eye rushes past the contemporary appearance into the
imaginative image of history or legend, situated by the adverbs "tunc,"
"quondam," "olim." The present condition of the arches seems almost
irrelevant to the contemplation of their once magnificent function. In still
other texts, Petrarch's historical vision strives unsuccessfully to discern the
tokens of a prestigious past now concealed too effectively by the modern
landscape. This at any rate seems to be the case when, as the verse letter to
Virgil describes it, Petrarch visited supposedly Virgilian haunts near Mantua:

Hinc tibi composui quae perlegio, otia nactus
Ruris amica tui; quonam vagus avia calle
Fusca sequi, quibus in pratis errare soleres
Assidue mecum volvens, quam fluminis oram
Quae curvi secreta lacus, quas arboribus umbras,
Quas nemorum latebras collisque sedilia parvi
Ambieris, cuius fessus seu cespitis herbam
Presseris accubitu, seu ripam fontis amoeni;
Atque ea praesentem mihi te spectacula reddunt.

(It is in this city [Mantua] that I have composed what you now
are reading. It is here that I have found the friendly repose of
thy rural fields. I constantly wonder by what path you were
wont to seek the unfrequented glades in thy strolls, in what
fields were wont to roam, what streams to visit, or what recess
in the curving shores of the lake, what shady groves and forest
fastnesses. Constantly I wonder where it was that you rested
upon the sloping sward, or that, reclining in moments of fa-

tigue, you pressed with your elbow the grassy turf or upon the
marge of a charming spring. Such thoughts as these bring you
back before my eyes.)

(*Familiares* 24.11)

At first the questing imagination seems to wander unappeased; and yet the
ultimate goal is attained, since Virgil's human presence emerges as a
reality—"praesentem"—even from the random questioning of stream and
wood.

The habit of seeking out everywhere the latent vestiges of history is
shared today by every tourist, but in Petrarch's century it was a momentous acquisition. His inquisitions of landscape reveal him in the act of
discovering history, and they reveal how creative, how inventive was this
act for which he is properly famous. The letters and poems that reflect the
exercise of his historical imagination exhibit him in the process of living
through this discovery, not only in his study but also in the daily experiences of his peripatetic life. To say that Petrarch "discovered" history
means, in effect, that he was the first to notice that classical antiquity was
very different from his own medieval world, and the first to consider
antiquity more admirable. Even if anticipations of these attitudes may be
found, he was the first to publicize them so effectively as to influence
profoundly his immediate posterity.

Thus Petrarch took more or less alone the step an archaic society must
take to reach maturity: he recognized *the possibility of a cultural alternative*.
With that step he established the basis of a radical critique of his culture:
not the critique that points to a subversion of declared ideals, but rather
the kind that calls ideals themselves into question. It is this immense shift
of perspective that is signaled by Petrarch's original way of looking at
places, and especially his view of Rome. Before him, writes Peter Burke,
the Roman ruins were noticed, but their historical significance was scarcely
perceived. "They were thought of as 'marvels,' *mirabilia*. But they were
taken as given. People seem not to have wondered how they got there,
when they were built, or why the style of architecture was different from
their own. The most they will do is to tell 'just so stories' or explanatory
myths about the names of places." With the rare exception of such a
protohumanist as Hildebert de Lavardin, this statement is true; its accuracy can be measured by the continuing use, well after the age of Petrarch,
of the twelfth-century "guidebook" *Mirabilia urbis Romae*, whose min-
gling of Christian miracle and topographic error betokens an incapacity or
unwillingness to perceive the passage of history. To gauge the originality

of Petrarch, one can set against the *Mirabilia* the extended passage in book 8 of the *Africa* that evokes the edifices of republican Rome with loving detail and reverent prolixity, even if not with archaeological precision. It was this Rome that Petrarch had gone to see and did see, despite the hostility of "present reality."

The effort of the imagination that produced these pages of the *Africa* reversed, in a sense, the imaginative effort behind the eighth book of the *Aeneid*—and to a lesser extent the treatment of place throughout that poem. For the *Aeneid* systematically introduces places as yet unfamiliar to its heroes but deeply charged for the Roman reader: Actium and Carthage, Cumae and Avernus, the Forum and the Janiculum. The *Aeneid* requires of its reader a simultaneous double vision that superimposes the past land-scape on the present, thus providing a peculiar pleasure compacted of recognition and nostalgia. This process is sustained most continuously in lines 337–61 of book 8, lines that follow Evander and Aeneas as they walk from the Carmental shrine to what was to become the Forum, and that stress repeatedly the modest pastoral simplicity of each hallowed site:

> Hinc ad Tarpeiam sedem et Capitolia ducit
> aurea nunc, olim silvestribus horrida dumis

> (From there he conducted them to Tarpeia's Place and the Capitol, which is now all gold, but was once wild and ragged, covered with woodland undergrowth.)

> (*Aeneid* 8.347–48)

The reader is required to hold before his eyes two plans, two histori-cal incarnations at once, and to shift his focus so quickly from the upper to the lower and back again that he grasps with a thrill the staggering impetus of time. Petrarch's eighth book makes no explicit reference to the city of his own age, to the Capitol once again "silvestribus horrida dumis," but the late medieval reader could not fail to perceive the Rome of the *Africa* as an archaeological construct. He would retrace in his mind the same promenade taken by the poet and Giovanni Colonna: he would superimpose present decay upon past glory and measure now the ironies of history. More painfully, he would confront a cultural alternative that appeared to dwarf his own crude and divided Christendom. For Petrarch, refusing Hildebert's conception of a fortunate Roman fall—"Maior sum pauper divite, stante iacens (I am greater in poverty than in wealth, prostrate than erect)"—saw the vestigial text of the Roman palimpsest as still more precious than its rude overlay.

Similar uses of landscape appear elsewhere in Petrarch's work where history is not at issue. The beautiful canzone that begins "Chiare fresche e dolci acque" (Canzone 126) situates the speaker in a landscape by a stream where once he had seen Laura bathing and where he repeatedly returns to recapture this privileged moment. He even pictures her, in his fantasy, returning some day to seek *him*, only to find his grave. The poem thus depends on two distinct superpositions of presence upon absence, past upon present. Several of the poems *in morte* will also represent the poet seeking and finding Laura present in the places she once frequented:

> Così comincio a ritrovar presenti
> le tue bellezze a' suoi usati soggiorni.

(Thus I begin to discover again the presence of your beauty in its accustomed haunts.)

(Canzone 282, ll. 7–8)

Fantasies like these constitute a kind of erotic, or perhaps narcissistic, complement to the fanciful re-creation of a historical site.

To move from these uses of the actual landscape to less literal interests and unearthings was only a small step for Petrarch, as it would be for the humanist movement he unknowingly fathered. The image that propelled the humanist Renaissance and that still determines our perception of it, was the archaeological, necromantic metaphor of *disinterment*, a digging up that was also a resuscitation or a reincarnation or a rebirth. The discovery of the past led men literally to dig in the ground, and the recovery from it of a precious object needed only a touch of fancy to be regarded as a resurrection. But the resurrection of buried objects and buildings could not be sharply distinguished from the resurrection of literary texts as they were discovered, copied, edited, disseminated, translated, and imitated by the humanist necromancer-scholar. Petrarch found it natural to use the term *ruinae* for the lost or fragmentary literary remains of antiquity, and he himself would be praised by later humanists for having brought the Latin language back to the light of day from among the ruins with which it had been entombed.

This commonplace Renaissance equation between the literal unearthing of antiquities and the unearthing or resurrection of ancient culture was already current during Petrarch's lifetime. Benvenuto of Vicenza (died 1323) celebrated the discovery of a manuscript of Catullus by composing a poem "de resurectione Catulli poete Veronensis." Boccaccio employed the same metaphor in at least three separate contexts in order to praise three great trecento artists: Dante, Giotto, and Petrarch himself. Filippo Villani, writing a short time after Petrarch's death, praised Giotto for having "revived the bloodless and almost extinct art of painting." Several passages in Petrarch's work can be associated with the same image. Thus the effort to decipher and recreate the buried reality of a place can be assimilated to the re-creation of a culture that was buried in various literal and progressively figurative ways. The title of a work by Valla—"Repastinatio," a digging up again—might have been used appropriately for any number of humanist writings.

Vestigial traces of necromantic superstition are by no means absent from the awe that produced this imagery. We catch an echo of it in the canzone "Spirto gentil" (Canzone 53), which evokes a senile Rome overcome by sleep, to be awakened perhaps by the unnamed hero who is being addressed. The call for Rome's reawakening is followed immediately by a vision of the ancient walls, the tombs of Roman heroes, the entire ruined city, and the souls beneath the earth of the Scipios, Brutus, and Fabricius, hoping and rejoicing at the prospect of an imminent *renovatio*: "tutto quel ch'una ruina involve, / per te spera saldar ogni suo vizio (All that a ruin envelops, hopes through you to remedy every loss)." The allusions to an underworld of heroes and metaphoric portraits of a stupefied or widowed Rome waiting to be revived, contain in germ the full-blown necromantic imagery of the later Renaissance. Petrarch, like Boccaccio, situated the otherness of the past beneath his feet and formulated his hopes of renewal in terms of a return to life.

The force of the necromantic superstition at the heart of the humanist enlightenment gave rise to a curious artistic phenomenon. It produced buildings and statues and poems that have to be scrutinized for subterranean outlines or emergent presences or ghostly reverberations. Renaissance art requires us to penetrate its visual or verbal surface to make out the vestigial form below, a revived classical form or a medieval form transmuted by a classicizing taste. Sir Kenneth Clark remarks that the Venus of Botticelli's *Primavera* "raises her hand with a gesture of a Virgin Annunciate; and the figure of Spring, fleeing from the icy embraces of the East Wind, is a Gothic nude." Anthony Blunt, discussing Lescot's design for the facade of the Cour Carrée of the Louvre, points out that the "triple repetition of the pavilion seems to be an echo, probably unconscious, of the late medieval chateau facade divided by three round towers, to be seen for instance at Josselin or Martainville."

Other examples from the visual arts would be easy to find. But it is above all the humanist literature of the Renaissance that requires an "archaeological" scrutiny, a decipherment of the latent or hidden or indecipherable object of historical knowledge beneath the surface. I propose to call this activity *subreading*. In the case of Petrarch, we can follow the ways in which subreading the landscape came to resemble subreading a culture. The crucial moment occurs when the poet turns from landscape to the literary remains of antiquity and struggles to pierce their verbal surfaces to reach the living particularity of the past they bear within them. This subreading seems to me to be a central activity of Petrarch's mind, an activity that can be distinguished from medieval hermeneutics and that he bequeathed to his humanist heirs.

Subreading an ancient text involved first of all an intuition of its otherness, an intuition that neither filial reverence nor fraternal affection could altogether dim. It also involved a dynamic and continuous interplay between the reader and the distant voice whose very accent and idiom he sought to catch. The first and essential discipline created by the humanist movement was the science of philology, which was designed to deal systematically with the otherness and distinctiveness of ancient literature. Philology, queen of the *studia humanitatis*, testified to the humanist discovery that cultural styles and verbal styles alter with time, like languages. Thus the first problem for the humanist was to deal with the temporal, cultural, and stylistic gap between the text and himself. Fully to bridge that gap required an effort of subreading that would unearth the alien presence carried by a text in all its subtle integrity. More arduous even than the reading of ruins is the intimate, delicate, and subtle conversation with a voice of the ancient past. The subreader tries to catch the inflections of a remote idiom, the cultural and personal quiddities obscured by millennial history. Petrarch's own capacity to subread is proven by his distinction as a gifted textual scholar. Writing to Boccaccio about the cult of Virgil on the part of Giovanni Malpaghini, his copyist and an aspiring poet, he remarks that he understands the seduction that the young man feels, rapt with the sweetness of another's wit—"alieni dulcedine raptus ingenii." We will not greatly distort the meaning of this phrase if we link the sweetness with the *alien* character of Virgil's genius. Petrarch himself was perhaps the first modern man to be intoxicated by this sweetness.

The reading of poetry before Petrarch had been described in terms of a different activity: not the bridging of time but the piercing of a veil. The activity of subreading needs to be distinguished from the conventional medieval hermeneutic methods with which it would at first coexist and which it would later progressively replace. It resembles neither the fourfold method of scriptural exegesis adapted by Dante and described in his letter to Can Grande, nor the Alexandrian method that presumed a poetic truth concealed by an allegorical veil. Petrarch himself echoes this latter presumption in several works, including his coronation address and the ninth book of the *Africa*: "sub ignoto tamen ut celentur amictu, / nuda alibi, et tenui frustrentur lumina velo ([Poets may] conceal in an unfamiliar garment things which otherwise are bare, and may baffle our vision with a fine veil," 9.100–101). But he also expressed doubts about the propriety of this presumption in the intrepretation of Virgil: once through the mouth of Augustinus in the *Secretum*, and again at greater length in the late letter to Federico Aretino containing an allegorical interpretation of the *Aeneid*, which he there assigns to his youth and which he is no longer prepared to support. Petrarch never explicitly recognized the disparity between the traditional hermeneutic presumptions and the presumptions that emerge in other works of his, most notably in the three letters on imitation (*Familiares* 1.8, 22.2, 23.19). But we can perceive these rhetorical and philological presumptions silently challenging the allegorical in his own mind, as we can follow this challenge or tension or split dividing humanist theory of the next two centuries.

The two hermeneutics are by no means mutually exclusive, but they do bring sharply dissimilar expectations to the literary text. The older method presupposed a fullness of knowledge awaiting the successful interpreter—knowledge that is whole and entire because it can be unlocked by a single operation of the appropriate intellectual key. This method aligned author and reader in a single universe of discourse wherein no cultural distance could exist because, with the sole exception of the Christian revelation, historical change was virtually unknown. The new "archaeological" hermeneutic, on the other hand, presupposed a considerable distance and withheld a single all-divulging key. Instead of a relation between "veil" and "truth" that, once discovered, is easily grasped and formulated, there emerges an interplay of entities that resists total description because it operates in the elusive domain of style. Style by definition cannot be described perfectly even if it can be categorized. And the poetic substance enmeshed in, or half-buried beneath, the verbal surface is now perceived as reaching the reader from far off, from a remote and prestigious world radically unlike his own.

Examples of the older method are not difficult to find in the corpus of Petrarch's work. One of the least convincing is the allegoristic wrenching of Virgil's first eclogue. In this particular instance, the effort of subreading failed; misled by a risky hermeneutic convention, Petrarch's literary intelligence could not locate the alien poetic substance latent in the words on his codex. The reductive hermeneutic presuppositions that underlay his gloss were supported by reverend authority and would continue to exercise an influence on literary theory as late as the seventeenth century. But their influence on the actual composition of poetry would decline sharply after the trecento, and Petrarch himself followed them systematically only in his *Bucolicum carmen*.

What in fact Petrarch did choose repeatedly to do as poet was to write verse that could itself be subread and demanded to be subread, verse bearing within it the latent presence of an ancient author. In so doing, of course, he again anticipated the course of the humanist imagination. We move here from the humanist subreading of an ancient text to the subreading required by a modern humanist text. Each activity, though distinct, can illuminate the other. The composition of humanist poetry can best be approached through the theory of imitation. Petrarch's fullest and most interesting discussion of it occurs in the letter to Boccaccio already cited (*Familiares* 23.19), which begins by portraying Giovanni Malpaghini. Petrarch goes on to describe himself as pleased with Giovanni's poetic progress but fearful that too crude a fidelity to their common master Virgil might vitiate his verse:

> Curandum imitatori, ut quod scribit simile non idem sit, eamque similitudinem talem esse oportere, non qualis est imaginis ad eum cuius imago est, quae quo similior eo maior laus artificis; sed qualis filii ad patrem, in quibus cum magna saepe diversitas sit membrorum, umbra quaedam et quem pictores nostri aerem vocant, qui in vultu inque oculis maxime cernitur, similitudinem illam facit, quae statim viso filio patris in memoriam nos reducat, cum tamen si res ad mensuram redeat, omnia sint diversa; sed est ibi nescio quid occultum quod hanc habeat vim. Sic et nobis providendum, ut cum simile aliquid sit, multa sint dissimilia, et idipsum simile lateat, nec deprehendi possit, nisi tacita mentis indagine, ut intelligi simile queat potius quam dici. Utendum igitur ingenio alieno, utendumque coloribus, abstinendum verbis. Illa enim similitudo latet, haec eminet. Illa poetas facit, haec simias.

> (A proper imitator should take care that what he writes resemble the original without reproducing it. The resemblance should not be that of a portrait to the sitter—in that case the closer the

likeness is the better—but it should be the resemblance of a son to his father. Therein is often a great divergence in particular features, but there is a certain suggestion, what our painters call an "air," most noticeable in the face and eyes, which makes the resemblance. As soon as we see the son, he recalls the father to us, although if we should measure every feature we should find them all different. But there is a mysterious something there that has this power. Thus we writers must look to it that with a basis of similarity there should be many dissimilarities. And the similarity should be planted so deep that it can only be extricated by quiet meditation. The quality is to be felt rather than defined. Thus we may use another man's conceptions and the color of his style, but not his words. In the first case the resemblance is hidden deep; in the second it is glaring. The first procedure makes poets, the second makes apes.)

(*Familiares* 23.19)

In this admirable passage, more enlightened than most discussions of the subject by later theorists, Petrarch is describing an object of knowledge that, unlike the "truth" represented by medieval allegory, cannot by definition be fully and succinctly delimited. The resemblance of a poem to its model or series of models will never be fully articulated, even supposing that it will be fully grasped. Rather, one subreads, patiently and intuitively, the dim, elusive presence of the model in the modern composition. This presence can no more be circumscribed than can the mysterious resemblance of a son to a father, or the confused relations between the levels of a buried city. Petrarch himself says this in one crucial sentence of the passage just quoted: "Sic et nobis providendum, ut cum simile aliquid sit, multa sint dissimilia, et idipsum simile lateat, nec deprehendi possit, nisi tacita mentis indagine, ut intelligi simile queat potius quam dici." This silent searching of the mind, "tacita mentis indagine," is considered never to complete its meditative investigation. That is because the object of knowledge is perceived to be composed not by a kernel of moral, religious, or philosophic wisdom, but by what might be called a *moral style*—a texture of feeling, thought, rhetoric, and tone defining itself allusively against a ground of literary tradition.

Petrarch's letter itself needs to be subread since its central comparison—likening the goal of proper literary imitation to the resemblance of a son to his father—bears just this resemblance to a much briefer simile in Seneca. . . . As we subread the father's features, indistinctly but unmistak-

ably, in his son's, so we subread Seneca in this letter, and so we subread
Virgil in the *Africa* and other poems. We pursue the diffused, the incomplete, the latent, even as we recognize that their presence cannot fully be
violated by verbal definition. Petrarch points to this fleeting latency when
he uses the word's etymological ancestor: "ut . . . idipsum simile lateat."
The interplay between the surface text and the antecedent or subtext
involves subtle interpenetrations, an interflowing and tingeing, an exchange of minute gradations, that cannot be measured wholly or formulated. If the allegorical meaning participated in being, the humanist interplay
is forever becoming. Reading and subreading it means dealing with the
implicit, the incipient, the virtual, and the inexpressible—"ut intelligi simile
queat potius quam dici."

The humanist poet's interplay with antiquity also involves what might
be called a subreading of the self. As Petrarch warned Malpaghini, the very
sweetness of otherness constitutes a risk, since it may change the poet into
an ape; it may so fill the spirit with another's presence that one's own
selfhood will be dimmed. Here he seems to adumbrate the idea that true
respect for another's wit requires a certain reciprocity. As the ultimate
symbols of this reciprocity, we might take his epistles in prose and verse to
the ancient authors who mattered most to him, epistles that characteristically reflect a certain humility but do not lack traces of their author's pride
and, in the case of Cicero, his disapproval. Petrarch read (and subread) the
ancients with less risk, with fuller appreciation, and with sharper philological acuity than Malpaghini not only because he was a great poet but also
because he was a great egoist. This means that he brought to his reading a
mind blessed with or condemned to compulsive self-questioning, a mind
greedy of experience and quick to change its tenor, a mind forever in the
process of becoming, obsessed with its own movements and turnings but
intermittently open nonetheless to other minds and worlds.

If Petrarch was the first great humanist, his primacy can teach us that
the fullest apprehension of otherness requires a continuous circle of adjustments. The subject who attempts to subread must be ready to play with
subjective styles of perception, must question and test himself as he sharp-
ens his intuitions, must finally subread his own consciousness to discern
that inner likeness, that virtual disposition capable of conversing with a
voice from the depths of time. Only thus can he taste without risk that
sweetness of the alien that will wither the unguarded and the pallid self.
Renaissance anthologies are full of poems by the Malpaghinis, who never
mastered this humanist circle of continuing adjustments. In the poetry of

mature humanism, subreading the alien text required subreading the range of potential styles of response in one's innermost being, imitation with the inner ear and then imitation with the pen. Imitation at its most powerful pitch required a profound act of self-knowledge and then a creative act of self-definition. Of course the reverse requirement is equally stringent: the definition or creation of literary voices, literary styles, required the progressive apprehension of voices and styles from outside the self.

This process of dynamic self-discovery is adumbrated in another, somewhat earlier letter to Boccaccio that also deals with imitation. Here the analogy is sartorial:

> Alioquin multo malim meus michi stilus sit, incultus licet atque horridus, sed in morem toge habilis, ad mensuram ingenii mei factus, quam alienus, cultior ambitioso ornatu sed a maiore ingenio profectus. . . . Omnis vestis histrionem decet, sed non omnis scribentem stilus; suus cuique formandus servandusque est, ne . . . rideamur. Et est sane cuique naturaliter, ut in vultu et gestu, sic in voce et sermone quiddam suum ac proprium, quod colere et castigare quam mutare cum facilius tum melius atque felicius sit.

> (I much prefer that my style be my own, rude and undefined, perhaps, but made to the measure of my mind, like a well-cut gown, rather than to use someone else's style, more elegant, ambitious, and ornamented, but suited to a greater genius than mine. . . . An actor can wear any kind of garment; but a writer cannot adopt any kind of style. He should form his own and keep it, for fear . . . we should laugh at him. Certainly each of us has naturally something individual and his own in his utterance and language as in his face and gesture. It is better and more rewarding for us to develop and train this quality than to change it.)

> (*Familiares* 22.2)

The perfunctory and quite insincere formulas of modesty need not detain us, but the perception that literary composition requires a lucid estimate of the self is important and valuable, and cuts deeper than the corresponding passage in Quintilian. Petrarch sees that a man's style is as personal as his face, and that both reflect the essential core of selfhood—

"quiddam suum ac proprium"—that makes him unique. Only after grasping his own selfhood can the artist create ("formare") and preserve his literary style. Actually, the conception of selfhood shifts slightly but significantly in the course of this passage. The sartorial analogy implies a conception that is basically static. The gown I wear either fits or fails to fit; I may choose between gowns but I cannot alter the fit once I put one on. But the argument that follows this analogy allows us to glimpse a more dynamic self-cultivation. By recognizing our capacity to develop and train ("colere et castigare") not only our style but also our essential individuality, Petrarch recognizes the potentially creative interplay between the alien and the self. Thus, for the humanist poet the beginning of creativity does not lie in a *cogito*, a *prise de conscience*, as it must, according to Georges Poulet, for the modern poet; it lies, rather, in a double groping—toward the otherness of the ancient text and toward a modern sensibility, a modern voice, that can mediate the ancient. And we as readers of humanist poems have to follow the interplay of that mediation, shifting our focus back and forth from the surface text to the fragments buried below it.

Thus these two letters on imitation can be made to yield a kind of embryonic theory of humanist composition, a theory that is clarified by other passages and other images in these same texts. Both letters make use of an apian analogy which was to become a humanist cliché but which in these Petrarchan contexts retains a fresh power of suggestion.

> Standum denique Senecae consilio, quod ante Senecam Flacci erat, ut scribamus scilicet sicut apes mellificant, non servatis floribus, sed in favos versis, ut ex multis et variis unum fiat, idque aliud et melius.

> (This is the substance of Seneca's counsel, and Horace's before him, that we should write as the bees make sweetness, not storing up the flowers but turning them into honey, thus making one thing of many various ones, but different and better.)
>
> *(Familiares* 23.19)

The familiar apian analogy implies a capacity for absorption and assimilation on the part of the poet, a capacity for making one's own the external text in all its otherness. That Petrarch did in fact perceive this process to be crucial in his own creative experience is clear:

Legi apud Virgilium apud Flaccum apud Severinum apud
Tullium; nec semel legi sed milies, nec cucurri sed incubui, et
totis ingenii nisibus immoratus sum; mane comedi quod sero
digererem, hausi puer quod senior ruminarem. Hec se michi
tam familiariter ingessere et non modo memorie sed medullis
affixa sunt unumque cum ingenio facta sunt meo, ut etsi
per omnem vitam amplius non legantur, ipsa quidem hereant,
actis in intima animi parte radicibus.

(I have read Virgil, Horace, Livy, Cicero, not once but a thousand times, not hastily but in repose, and I have pondered them
with all the powers of my mind. I ate in the morning what I
would digest in the evening; I swallowed as a boy what I would
ruminate upon as a man. These writings I have so thoroughly
absorbed and fixed, not only in my memory but in my very
marrow, these have become so much a part of myself, that even
though I should never read them again they would cling in my
spirit, deep-rooted in its inmost recesses.)

(Familiares 22.2)

Here the analogy is digestive, and it too can be traced back to Seneca as
well as forward at least to Francis Bacon, but the formulation here corresponds to something of moment in the poet's own artistic formation. It
betokens an intimacy of conversation with the ancient text, a habitual
interiorization of its letter and essence, and a freedom to transform, to
recreate this sweetness of an alien wit into the honey of one's own
personal creation.

One might argue that already in these digestive and apian analogies
there lies in germ the obsessive analogy of a rebirth. The metamorphosis of
the ancient into renewed modern life within the poet's consciousness
constitutes a kind of renascence. This metamorphic implication is more
visible in a much earlier usage of the bee simile:

Neve diutius apud te qualia decerpseris maneant, cave: nulla
quidem esset apibus gloria, nisi in aliud et in melius inventa
converterent. Tibi quoque, siqua legendi meditandique studio
repperis, in favum stilo redigenda suadeo.

(Take care that the nectar does not remain in you in the same

state as when you gathered it; bees would have no credit unless
they transformed it into something different and better. Thus if
you come upon something worthy while reading or reflecting,
change it into honey by means of your style.)

(*Familiares* 1.8)

Petrarch seems already to see that this kind of assimilation must occur if
the modern text is truly to recall its paternal model imprecisely but
unmistakably. Only this profounder and more secret act of "imitation"
permits the authentic subreading of a latent otherness in the modern work
and invests it with its unique historical depth. The alien text has been
absorbed so thoroughly that its presence *haunts* the polyvocal modern text,
slowly reveals itself to the silent searching of the mind, resonates faintly
in the third ear. In that resonance lies its renascence. The reader divines a
buried stratum, as a visitor to Rome divines the subterranean foundations
of a temple.

In Petrarch's own poetry, this latent stratum can be felt only intermittently, and more commonly in the Latin works than in the vernacular.
Neither body is lacking in pseudoimitation, in perfunctory assimilation
and distorted self-definition. Most noticeably, the *Africa* is marred by
failings that from our perspective can be attributed to a double incapacity:
first, to grasp the alien substance of ancient epic in its artistic fullness; and
second, to gauge lucidly the character of the writer's own poetic vocation.
In fact, Petrarch's most successful and influential poetry needs to be subread
less consistently than does the poetry of his great humanist successors—
Poliziano and Tasso, Ronsard and du Bellay, Jonson and Milton, among
them. Yet there are instances of "imitation" in something like the creative
sense we have been considering, and these instances, however scattered
and brief, are full of interest; in terms of the history of European poetry,
they are highly significant.

The poetry initiated by Petrarch in these scattered instances was to
become a major current of Renaissance literature, a current whose signal
successes amid the perennial mediocrity proved that the double quest of
the humanist artist could fecundate the imagination. Before the current
spent itself, Petrarch's poetry was itself to achieve the status of a classic;
after the dead poetic interval of the earlier quattrocento, and after the
genuine poetic renewal of the full European Renaissance, his work joined
the ancients' as the object of innumerable attempted resuscitations, some
of them splendidly successful. The poems of this current, enriched by a
new and subtle polyvocality, might be described as *chronomachias*, battle-

grounds for a conflict of eras, a struggle of period styles. In an authentic struggle, the contemporary always wins—which is to say that the poetic voice learns from the baptism of otherness to find its own unique salvation. Merleau-Ponty has written:

> L'histoire vraie vit . . . tout entière de nous. C'est dans notre présent qu'elle prend la force de remettre au présent tout le reste. L'autre que je respecte vit de moi comme moi de lui. Une philosophie de l'histoire ne m'ôte aucun de mes droits, aucune de mes initiatives. Il est vrai seulement qu'elle ajoute à mes obligations de solitaire celle de comprendre d'autres situations que la mienne, de créer un chemin entre ma vie et celle des autres, c'est-à-dire de m'exprimer.

It was this arduous route that the great humanists of the Renaissance chose—and Petrarch first of all—in their momentous search for a self-expression that was, then as always, self-discovery.

Petrarch's *search* for self-discovery was complicated by the division, narcissism, and volatility of that self. As one moves from his conceptions of imitation to his poetic practice, these particularities of his personality intrude themselves as constituent elements of his writing. Quite possibly the discovery of history came the more readily to him because he was by birth a dislocated individual. His parents were already in exile in Florence when he was born in Arezzo; much of his youth and maturity were spent in and around Avignon, site of the "exiled" holy See. Thus Petrarch was born deracinated, and while young was marked by that "avara Babilonia" which mingled and corrupted indifferently men of various estates and tongues. Petrarch did not frequently refer to this uprooting, but we can judge its importance to him from the tears shed by Franciscus when the subject arises in the *Secretum*. "Are you unaware," he asks Augustinus, "of this stepmother Fortune's cruelty, which in a single day destroyed with one brutal stroke all my hopes and wealth, my family and home?" (Illa ne tibi inaudita est Fortune novercantis immanitas, cum uno die me spesque et opes meas omnes et genus et domum impulsu stravit impio?) Avignon anticipated the modern city in its power to cut men off from their *attachments* to a class, a place, and a community. Petrarch grew up without strong attachments of this sort, without a ceremonial identity, and his bookish genius transformed a dislocation in space into a dislocation in time, into a nostalgia for a City that was not Florence but rather the Rome of the republic.

This dislocation appears to have been one of the factors that heightened his self-perception. On the opening page of *De remediis ultriusque fortune* appears a quotation from Saint Miniato that treats the problem of self-consciousness in a peculiarly modern spirit.

> I see that nature has provided all irrational animals with a remarkable protection, namely a lack of knowledge of themselves; only to us who are human do I see memory, intelligence, and foresight turned into torment and weariness.

The sense of time, the possession of three faculties corresponding to the three realms of earthly temporality, permits that reflexive capacity to examine our selves and our conduct which makes us responsible and problematic animals. The exacerbated self-consciousness is of a piece with the intensified historical consciousness—the two sources of that originality which, quite apart from his poetic gifts, constitute Petrarch's signal importance in the history of the European mind. As the quest for a community was displaced from the geographical frame to the historical, ceremonial absolutes were undermined by the recognition of alternatives, and through the dawning perception of cultural otherness there emerged new criteria for judgment, including self-judgment. The opacity of the other, the distinct particularity of the other, led to a recognition of the uniqueness of the self which ceremonial symbolism could not represent. The rootless, self-questioning personality, half in love with and half perplexed by its reflexive inquisitions, was haunted by Fortune as Chronos, by the privations of mutability and the enormous holocaust of history. There may have been a fatality in the fact that the earliest diachronic poetry of the modern era, the first poetry deliberately to dramatize the passage of history, would dramatize a descent into a selfhood unsure of its status.

In the writing of Petrarch this lack of assurance affected that vocation for historical mediation, for what I have called transitivity, which he felt quite as strongly as had his Roman masters. Petrarch refers in several contexts to his felt responsibility as interpreter of the classical heritage not so much or not only for his contemporaries as for posterity. In an early letter (*Familiares* 1.9) he calls this task a form of charity ("charitas"). Later passages return to the theme with varying degrees of hopefulness. There were indeed grounds for qualifying the hope. The effort of mediation, which Petrarch correctly understood to be creative, would require a complex set of gifts involving a patient and subtle discipline. It would require what Nietzsche called the plastic power (*plastische Kraft*) enabling a man to assimilate and make healthy use of history. The ideal of mediation lacks in itself any hint of the means whereby a passive inheritance is rendered transitive; it lacks the magic formula by which humanist turns necromancer. The whole enterprise, the whole drama of Petrarch's humanism centers on the effort to win through to hermeneutic and creative responses that could deal productively with ancient literature in something vaguely resembling its own terms. His effort was inhibited by his intrusive egoism and deracinated loyalties, which, if they led him to momentous new experiences, troubled his capacity to control them.

One may set against the relatively confident passages of the letters on imitation the following sonnet (Canzone 40) alluding to a specific but unnamed imitative work (the *Africa?* the *De viris illustribus?*) for which the writer needs a certain manuscript in the possession of the sonnet's Roman addressee.

> S'amore o morte non dà qualche stroppio
> a la tela novella ch' ora ordisco,
> e s' io mi svolvo dal tenace visco,
> mentre che l'un coll'altro vero accoppio,
>   i' farò forse un mio lavor sí doppio
> tra lo stil de' moderni e 'l sermon prisco
> che, paventosamente a dirlo ardisco,
> infin a Roma n'udirai lo scoppio.
>   Ma però che mi manca a fornir l'opra
> alquanto de la fila benedette
> ch'avanzaro a quel mio diletto padre,
>   perché tien' verso me le man sí strette
> contra tua usanza? I' prego che tu l'opra,
> e vedrai riuscir cose leggiadre.

(If Love or Death does not cut short the new cloth that now I prepare to weave, and if I loose myself from the tenacious birdlime while I join one truth with the other, I shall perhaps make a work so double between the style of the moderns and ancient speech that [fearfully I dare to say it]

you will hear the noise of it even as far as Rome. But, since I
lack, to complete the work, some of the blessed threads that
were so plenteous for that beloved father of mine, why do you
keep your hands so closed toward me, contrary to your cus-
tom? I beg you to open, and you will see delightful things
result.)

The declaration of a humanist poetic intent is qualified by the conditional
phrases of the first quatrain and the "forse" (perhaps) of line 5. If it
survives the threats of love and death, the work to come will consist of a
fabric ("tela") made from two interwoven styles historically dissimilar
(Christian modern and ancient classical) which correspond to two structures of truth. To finish, the writer requires a text by a beloved father
(Livy? Augustine?) that he now lacks. The fabric of the father's work is to
be undone, ravelled out, so that only its blessed threads remain to be
rewoven in a new design and then to be subread later within a tissue
altogether new. If it suffers no rip ("stroppio"), the result of this interweaving will be so original as to cause a splash, an explosion ("scoppio,"
l. 8) that, the writer adds with express timidity, may be audible even in
Rome. Whereas the metaphorical shifts of the letters on imitation seem to
succeed each other more or less harmoniously, this sonnet offers a series
of metaphors not easily accommodated. The single verb *accoppiare*
(l. 4) means "to couple, to marry, to pair, to yoke." Which emphasis
should the reader choose? Is the act of imitative acculturation a serene
marriage, a sexual union, a forcible yoking of animals or their violent
breeding? How smoothly are the two truths wedded in this double labor?
The primary meaning of the metaphoric "visco" (l. 3)—birdlime, snare—is
apparently the passion for Laura to which "l'amore" (l. 1) also refers, but
the presentation of the "visco" as something distinct from "amore"
suggested by the conjunction "e" (l. 3) and the proximity of this sticky
trap to the act of coupling in line 4 suggest a more generalized snare
inherent in this act. The concluding word, "leggiadre"—"graceful, delightful"—has to be reconciled with the force of "scoppio" (l. 8). The filial
metaphor evoking the spiritual father appears in a context locating the
father as absent in that mythical, unattainable city where perhaps only
explosions can reach him. Simultaneous filiation and lack, confidence and
apprehension, freedom and claustration, harmony and violence, suggest
that the actual imitative texts Petrarch produced would disclose his own
ambivalences. The texts do indeed reveal various antithetical pulls; but

they are not necessarily crippled works of art for thus exposing their tensions. *Virescit vulnere virtus*. At their strongest, Petrarch's humanist poems fulfill their imitative impulse, authenticate their transitive function, while reflecting the private and historical vulnerability of their tormented author.

ALDO SCAGLIONE

Classical Heritage and Petrarchan Self-Consciousness in the Literary Emergence of the Interior "I"

Since autobiography inevitably looms large in the background of the exposition which follows, I wish to open with a brief discussion of the matter according to the recent speculation on this now rather fashionable genre. We have been witnessing in recent years a lively interest in autobiography which specialists date from the first landmark study by the French historian of philosophy, Georges Gusdorf, in the miscellany *Formen der Selbstdarstellung*, which has evolved through other studies such as those by, first and foremost, Roy Pascal, as well as others by Wayne Shumaker, Karl J. Weintraub, James Olney, Northrop Frye and Georg Misch. The difficulty of definition was ironically highlighted by a sort of minor accident: when Jean Cocteau was invited to contribute an essay to that same miscellany, he replied that everything he wrote was autobiographical. Salvador Dali is one who, if asked for another self-portrait, could certainly have asserted that all his painting was as autobiographical as a self-portrait. One could even plausibly, and only half facetiously, assert that Picasso's constant turning out of rotund forms in all styles was at least in part a transformed mirror-image of his own self. Indeed, when we try to understand the nature of autobiography we invariably end up with an elusive genre and a ubiquitous theme, hard to define precisely in literary terms and analysable in human terms only with the most abstract, even if at times penetrating generalities.

More recent research has rightly chosen to tackle the matter in a broader and more productive context, namely that of discovery of the self

From *Altro Polo*. © 1984 by the University of Sydney. Frederick May Foundation for Italian Studies, University of Sydney, 1984.

or self-consciousness, an epistemological, psychological and anthropological approach that transcends the literary genre without precluding the possibility of fastening on literary and artistic qualities. Indeed, Georges Gusdorf specifically concluded that the last critical phase in our analysis of autobiography ought to be a consideration of its anthropological significance. Beyond the fallacy of searching for factual accuracy, and the literary-minded reader's search for artistic coherence, we find in true autobiography a symbol of an externalised consciousness, the creation of the self by the self. We end up with two distinct yet convergent phenomena: the literary genre of autobiography and the literary emergence of an analysis of the self or of the inner psyche as both a human and a literary event. In the course of studying the question, I have concluded that the two cannot really be separated.

We must start with some clear and broadly accepted definitions (the best of which to date are probably to be found in Roy Pascal), which will serve to separate the genre of autobiography from the broader theme of self-discovery. First, autobiography must have a plot, tell a story—the story of a life in the world. Hence it must be dramatic and relate an individual personality, seen from within, to its external world. It must, then, be both social and "private . . . secret . . . intimate." And the story must be made up of "concrete experienced reality" of the spiritual identity of the individual (Misch). If the narrative is not self-centred but rather other-centred, it makes not an autobiography but a memoir. Most political autobiographies belong more to that genre, except when the self, the individual politician, has acted out of a powerful spiritual motivation.

Since we are dealing with the story of a life, time becomes an essential ingredient. We are confronted with the relationship between past and present. This distinguishes autobiography from another allied genre or subgenre, namely the diary or personal chronicle. In this respect autobiography is a review of a life from a particular moment in time, with a coherent, retrospective *ex post facto* design, and also, although not coextensive with the former, an inner truth (or rather sincerity) which may be plainly contradictory to outer, objective truth. This covers several possible genres, yet it also excludes several, especially the diary or journal which moves through a prolonged chain of moments in time. The latter's message as to the meaning of life cannot therefore be planned coherently and intentionally beforehand, as in the autobiography: "Autobiography is," conclusively, "the shaping of the past. It imposes a pattern on a life, constructs out of it a coherent story." The centre is the self, but the world must be present, otherwise we cannot have real communicable experiences and the unfolding of a dramatic story. This excludes and partly disqualifies true mystical experiences. Yet the world is present, typically, only as the setting against which the personality arises and which forms and determines it. On the other hand, "the coherence of the story implies that the writer takes a particular standpoint, the standpoint of the moment at which he reviews his life, and interprets his life from it."

Because of the particular manner in which past and present interface in the autobiography, a sort of circularity obtains whereby, as it were, "the beginning is in the end, . . . the end in the beginning"; we get a "subtle penetration of the past by the present." We could say that Aristotle's definition of the plot as something having a beginning, a middle and an end acquires a special retrospective dimension, since while the progress from beginning to end is still chronologically there, psychologically it becomes reversed, or at least subjected to an inherent to-and-fro movement that distinguishes the genre. At the same time, an autobiography "is an artistic failure if . . . its end is assumed from the beginning": for example, when the story of a disabused communist makes us feel the coming disillusionment from the beginning, as in Arthur Koestler's autobiography.

At this point one can take a further step that virtually bridges the gap between autobiography and the broader literature of self-consciousness. For it is certain that an autobiography must decisively include "the meaning an event acquires when viewed in the perspective of a whole life." It lies in the very nature of autobiography that it gives meaning, a posteriori, to the chaotic and potentially absurd sequence of an individual's lifetime sensations and apprehensions of the infinitely unpredictable environmental setting; every event as selected and narrated by the autobiographer is given a meaning only within his or her whole life story, the general design of which is superimposed on the past at the moment of composition, the present. But one can see how, apart from this singular, global dimension, the essence of autobiography becomes the finding of consciousness of the self (*Selbstbesinnung*), which can also be, and in a sense always is, a fictional, imagined, objectified and distanced self like another character created by a narrator, or a lyrical detached poetic self. Lest we misunderstand the insistence on coherence, unity and design in the self-portrait, let us never forget that the self, and typically the self of a (good) autobiography is Protean like Rembrandt's sixty-two self-portraits or Dürer's self-representations in different symbolic roles, and unlike the biographers' portraits we find appended to autobiographies by editors, which are fixed, timeless and static, something which the autobiographer's self-portrait cannot and must not be.

To return to Aristotle, this time for his distinction between poetry and history: the autobiographer's history is not particular, but universal, not objective, but imaginary, not realistic, but symbolic. It re-presents the past not as it was, but as the autobiographer thinks it was, that is, as it might or should have been, from his/her point of view. For autobiography is memory, not reconstruction but interpretation. If we return to an earlier element of our definition, the need for privacy or secret intimacy, we see how autobiography clearly spills over into the broader area of self-consciousness beyond the genre, because the way the self emerges depends on psychological evolution and discoveries that are not limited to that genre. Montaigne's essays are not, by our definition, autobiography, since they lack a narrative plot, yet autobiographical they undoubtedly are, and the portraiture of the individual in the novel or in biography—a subgenre of historiography, quite remote from *auto*biography—clearly evolves in a way that reflects the growing and changing consciousness of the intimate, secret self.

We now reach a point of transition that determines our characterisation of the genre and its broad implications. That is, we must answer the question: is autobiography as we know it eternal and universal? The answer has been usually a firm negative. With some qualifications, all specialists seem to agree that autobiography is a Western European genre that started with St. Augustine's *Confessions*, and was thus tied to Christianity. Georg Misch, who produced the most detailed surveys of the genre, wrote two large volumes on pre-Christian ancient autobiography. Nevertheless he, along with others, tended to conclude that true autobiography came about as a result of the Christian revolution, with its unprecedented focussing on the individual inner man and the soul, and thus on the need and institutionalised practice of introspection, self-examination and confession. As St Bonaventure in the thirteenth century was to put it in his memorable formula *in te ipsum redi; transcende et te ipsum*, the Christian's turning away from the world to the self (*itinerarium in seipsum*) is the first stage of the movement to God (*itinerarium mentis ad Deum*).

If this is so, we are bound to wonder: is there no true autobiography outside Christian Europe? Has not Judaism produced autobiography? Does not the Bible contain autobiography? Perhaps the Book of Job? And does the introspection of the Christian not extend to that immediate offshoot of Christianity, Islam? Would there be anything equivalent to European autobiography in Oriental literature, perhaps through Christian influence, literary or broadly spiritual or psychological? If we grant, for example, that Buddhist or Taoist total concentration on the pure consciousness of the inner self does not qualify, because it rejects an essential ingredient, the sense of dramatic conversion through experience of evil in the space and time of the world (since Christian virtue is not pure, but a continuous struggle with Satan and sin), may we then exclude this broad geographic area from autobiography as a strictly defined genre? Most ancient as well as modern non-Christian autobiographies are of the "political," public kind, more like memoirs. However, Georg Misch, without denying his basic definition, certainly did not hesitate to give much space to such forms; according to Misch, self-descriptions of this kind do have a place in the history of autobiography, if one keeps this distinction in mind.

The question of individualism is highly relevant to autobiography. Aristotle, in *Politics* 6.7, observed that European tribes outside Greece were incapable of organisation into states because the strong individualism of their members could not be properly harnessed. On the other hand, Oriental populations reduced their entire cultural life to that of the state, with no room for the free expression of individuality. Only the Greeks were capable of combining both, the organised political life of the state alongside the free expression of individual values, although they refused to form units larger than necessary in order to make possible a rational political life. This evaluation is confirmed by Georges Gusdorf, who attributes the rise of autobiography to the change from the collectivism of archaic societies to the modern sense of individualism. We could say that Aristotle's summary perception can be applied, *mutatis mutandis*, to the contrast between the self in the autobiographical form on the three shores of the Mediterranean: the European Christian on the one side, and the African and Asian Islamic on the other. This comparison should be constructive for specialists of autobiography, in view of the fact that they have tended to restrict their surveys to Europe alone, with only a few samplings from other areas.

To return to my broader topic, namely that of the discovery of the self in any literary form, I should like to introduce the dramatis personae who will take us through several centuries. In order to place the concept in its proper perspective, one should start with that distant but ever-present ideal master of Western humanism, Socrates, who changed the course of Greek thought by maintaining that it had followed the wrong track. To put his message in the words of the eighteenth-century Italian philosopher Giambattista Vico, we can only know that which we have done; therefore nature and the physical world, which were made by God, cannot be the true object of man's investigation: only man's activity is a legitimate subject of philosophy and science. In Alexander Pope's words: "Know thyself then, presume not God to scan, / The proper study of mankind is man."

When ancient pagan culture was shaken to its foundations by Christianity's revelation of the inner, inalienable sanctity of the human person, endowed with an individual soul directly issuing from God Himself, St Augustine crystallised the revolutionary message in literary form by inventing the new genre of autobiography in his *Confessions*. There he told the story of his personal experience not as an ancient hero revelling in personal pride but in order to praise the Lord and raise a hymn to His all-encompassing mercy, for He had lifted a wretched and hopeless sinner to the glory of His Grace. It was only against this Christian background that the most refined (and yet most physically base) sentiment of man, that of love for a woman, thoroughly sensual and inescapably sexual throughout antiquity, could become sublimated into something almost completely ideal and spiritual. This marked the achievement of the Provençal troubadours, who in their verses shaped, as Denis de Rougemont has demonstrated, one of the few recorded real changes in the nature of human emotions, a change that could only be Christian inspired.

It is essential to keep in mind that this sublimated love is a form of discovery of the self. When we hear that the chivalric lovers of old were self-centred, or further that their passion was man-centred and did not do justice to the woman, who was not really taken into account, we hear only a modern polemical interpretation that is historically alien to the point under consideration here. The woman was not taken into account because the poet was inventing an abstract form of self-discovery, based on a sentiment or passion that did not need a personal object, so that, as has been repeatedly stressed, it is inappropriate to search for the historical or physical identity of a Beatrice, a Laura, a Fiammetta, since they were nothing but objectified, symbolic extensions of the poet's self. Dante Alighieri took it upon himself to carry the process of Provençal poetry to its most logical and radical conclusion by devising a mode of loving that not only excluded all physical aspects, but showed its purity and self-sufficiency by needing no reward at all from the beloved, not even the greeting. Indeed Beatrice became after her death his perfect love object, because then she was pure spirit and Dante's love could in no way be touched or diminished. It was Dante's way to make the experience totally internal, a concern of the autonomous self, absolutely intangible from the outside.

Petrarch combined the lesson of the troubadours with that of Dante by making his person the major theme of all his work, both in prose and verse, starting from the *Secretum* and ending with the *Canzoniere*. He did so in a way that distinguished him uniquely from both his predecessors and his contemporaries; he further spiritualised the love celebrated by the troubadours and set himself against Dante by making Laura not a way to God, as Beatrice had been, but the objective correlative of God, divinity on earth, the love of God descended into the creature. Petrarch's literary modes were also distinct from those of Boccaccio, just as the lyrical mode is distinct from and opposed to the narrative. In literature lyric connotes the subjective and the ego-centred, just as narrative connotes the objective and the other-centred. Petrarch, the lyric model par excellence of European literature, was always speaking about himself even when introducing characters, whether these were named Augustine, Scipio or Laura, whereas Boccaccio was speaking about other people as he saw them even when he was introducing himself as just another of his fictional characters (so that he can be, and has been, accused of "lying" in his alleged autobiographical stories).

Let us now take a closer look at what Petrarch achieved in the realm with which we are concerned. In order to do so his personality must be set against the background of earlier analyses of the ego. Concentration on the ego as a proper subject of attention was a problematic undertaking that could be viewed in two distinct ways. On the one hand the Pauline strain taught that the most capital of capital sins was that of yielding to the instinct that afflicts fallen man, the instinct to draw all interest to oneself, to place oneself at the centre, to give to oneself what is rightfully due to one's neighbour and to God—all of which amounts to pride. This Pauline strain remained, as we know, a strong pillar of Christian ethics, and even at the time of the High Renaissance it could surface with the power of a revolutionary thrust. Hence Luther logically and radically concluded that, repeating Augustine's words, all the virtues of the ancient and modern heroes are nothing but shining yet deceptive vices (*splendida vitia*): it is ruinous to hope for salvation through our deeds and good intentions, since these do nothing but nurture pride. It is therefore better for man to sin because this will cause him to be humble, and humility is the antidote of pride. Faith alone justifies, and the only truly unforgivable sin is pride. Following this line of reasoning, Augustine managed to write the story of his ego in a true Christian-Pauline key by beating his breast as a great sinner raised from the utmost baseness by God's Grace, thus becoming a humble egotist; the tables were turned and autobiography had avoided the pitfall of unforgivable egocentrism or narcissism. This special way of concentrating on the self became, indeed, the true Christian way.

Learning from the Socratic method of knowing oneself, yet avoiding the pagan anthropomorphism and anthropocentrism, it came to mean the method of withdrawing into the self away from the outer things of the world in order to be able to see God deep within oneself. For the Christian God is the God within. To put it, once again, according to the formula of St Bonaventure, which emanates from Augustine, the way of the Christian has two movements: first from externality to the intimacy of the self, then from the lowness of the self to the sublimity of God (*in te ipsum redi; transcende et te ipsum*).

Thus the autobiographic genre had been born in a paradox: the subject-object of analysis, the self, was presented in a negative and dialectical way; the self was put forward only to negate and transcend it. One of the great individualists before the Renaissance, Peter Abelard, produced a shining example of this literary predicament. His autobiography, the *Historia calamitatum*, was an act of confession and ascetic Christian self-accusation. A contrastive analysis between the *Historia calamitatum* and Petrarch's *Secretum* is most illuminating, for it throws light on the chasm that separates one of the most powerful medieval personalities from the "first modern man," as Petrarch has repeatedly been dubbed. In the dialogue of the *Secretum* Petrarch's interlocutor St Augustine accuses Petrarch of sloth, pride, vanity and lust, but Petrarch sees as *gloria* and *amor* what to Augustine appear as pride and lust. Petrarch is not sure that he can save himself from these propensities which are so deeply rooted in his soul, but he feels that the ancient virtues of love of glory and love of beauty cannot be mere *splendida vitia*, for they are his (human) way of using the talents that God has given him. His literary activity, his calling in life, grant him a legitimate claim to glory, and Laura is not an object of lustful desire but the inspirer of literary activity; she is the one who has made him a poet.

The year in which Petrarch was composing the final draft of the *Secretum* was around the time he planned the collection of his *Familiar Letters*, a true autobiographical document, and also the time when he drafted the fictitious letter on the ascent to Mont Ventoux. This letter was, in retrospect, a sort of programmatic manifesto for all of Petrarch's career: when he reached the summit of the mountain, the poet would have us believe that he casually opened the book of Augustine's *Confessions*, which he had brought along, and the book opened at the passage that read: "Et eunt homines admirari alta montium, et latissimos lapsus fluminum et gyros siderum, et relinquunt se ipsos [Men go out to admire the summits of the mountains, the broad waterfalls of mighty rivers, the vast expanse of the ocean, and the circling movement of the stars—and forget to look at their own selves]." Having reached the summit, writes Petrarch, he was contemplating the awesome spectacle of the vast horizon, from the Lyonese mountains to the sea of Marseilles all the way to Aiguesmortes with the Rhône down below. The detailed observation filled his mind now with higher thoughts, following by analogy the upward movement that had taken his body from the lowness of the plain to the height of the summit. He then opened the book of the *Confessions*, the reading of which made him angry with himself for not ceasing to be attracted by worldly things. He thus learned from Augustine what Augustine himself had learnt from Paul and St Anthony had learnt from the Gospel, that men are wanting because they neglect the noblest part of themselves and disperse their attention by turning to vain external spectacles.

The convergence, indeed confluence of these seemingly disparate documents, the *Secretum*, the letter of Mont Ventoux and the whole collection of the *Familiares*, indicate that Petrarch, by that time, had found the focus of his personality and literary career. This convergence was to constitute the ultimate expression of the laying open of his inner self to the world, a signal *exemplum* of Christian man in thought, feeling and action. The letter is a paradox, a paradox wherein lies the key to the much discussed inner conflicts of Petrarch, the man and the poet. He struggled all his life with the conflicts of desire for recognition and fame, even glory (in the republic of letters and the courts of the great) and the need for solitude for the sake of total concentration on his literary work. In this letter, we are caught by surprise when, after Petrarch has climbed a mountain apparently for its own sake, for the purpose of satisfying a human curiosity for a remote and forbidding aspect of physical nature, we find that the purpose of that earliest of all recorded alpine exploits was to reveal the vanity of curiosity, and to alert himself as well as his fellow humans to the fact that true wisdom lies in looking away from nature and the world. And yet we must not be deceived by the ascetic conclusion of the text for, and this is specifically relevant for our purpose, what Petrarch transmitted was not so much a "medieval" lesson in withdrawal from the world as a testimony of the power of spiritual qualities that are within ourselves. His search for God became de facto a discovery of the potentialities of the psyche, even with all its human limitations. In any event, the die was cast; the mould of his whole life was definitively sealed. He would go on living, as he had lived to that day, with his contradictions, doubts and fears, and would make peace with them, without hoping ever to resolve them. He would go on analysing himself and his conflicts without holding anything back, with ruthless honesty, in one of the most remarkable displays of clear-headedness ever recorded.

Throughout the whole of Petrarch's varied and extensive production there is not only the constant presence of the leading ideas of self-revelation and the search in the self for what constitutes civilised behaviour, but also a continuous, intricately intertwining recurrence of leitmotifs that variously and sometimes darkly symbolise those ideas. In a way we can say that no matter what literary genre Petrarch is handling, in any one of his hundreds of letters, poems, essays or treatises, he is always saying the same things in a different way. We then can ask ourselves: where did he learn that kind of coherence? I submit that the source of inspiration, the ever-present guide towards this goal was and could be none other than Dante. We all know, and Petrarch stated it without fear of sounding impertinent, that he did not agree with Dante. Their personalities were at opposite poles, and their aims were equally opposite. But this does not mean that he had no use for Dante, although he did not hesitate to imply as much. For one thing, he found in Dante an unprecedented example of a man whose several works formed a tightly-knit mosaic of analysis and correspondences, a constant search for the answers to the very questions already raised at the outset of this article. Dante's last work, the *Paradiso*, was the answer to the question raised in the first, the *Vita nuova*: namely how to praise his lady in a truly fitting way and in words that were never spoken of any woman. Even his technical treatises, such as the *De vulgari eloquentia* and *De monarchia*, were treatments and solutions of problems preliminary and internal to the *Divina commedia*. The *Convivio* contained the definition of a mode of reading the *Vita nuova*, the allegorical mode which supplied the necessary transition to the understanding of the *Commedia*. Likewise Petrarch's life impresses us from beginning to end with its absolute consistency, being firmly hinged on a complex yet admirably constant system of values, ideas and themes. One of these values is to be found in the very context of the letter on Mont Ventoux, and deserves our attention because it is central to Petrarchan poetics.

It is an enticing hypothesis to wonder whether the reason for that passage from Augustine being so indelibly imprinted on Petrarch's memory is that it is part of a long discussion on memory. Augustine's discussion of the unfathomable powers and boundaries of human memory was related to his search for God. According to Augustine, our idea of God is undoubtedly stored in our memory as a logical consequence of our unquenchable thirst for a happiness which cannot be based on anything we have experienced in this world or received through our senses, whereas the unlimited remainder of what is stored in the memory derives from the senses. His argument proceeds by elimination, and concludes that, since it is based on the presence of God within us, our idea of happiness cannot come from the objects of sensual experience, just as happiness itself cannot derive from sensual things but only from what is already within our spirit. The notion of memory is an integral part of Petrarch's method, practice and theory. To begin with, it has been noted (for instance, by Adelia Noferi) that Petrarch displays an incapacity to live except through the memory of the past and the anticipation of a vague future—which, on the other hand, conflicts with his conviction that wisdom lies in the capacity to enjoy the present.

There is a passage at the beginning of the *Epistola posteritati* whose full meaning within our context seems to have escaped the attention of the critics. Petrarch writes:

> My youth deluded me, my younger manhood led me astray, but my old age corrected me by teaching me through the experience of what I had read long before: that youth and pleasure are nothing but vanity. Rather, the Creator of all ages corrected me, He who sometimes allows the vainly proud mortals to err in order to make them know themselves through the recollection, though late, of their sins.

Memores and *se cognoscant* in the original Latin are key words, linking memory and self-knowledge: indeed the latter is dependent on the former, the key precept of Socratic humanism. His *revisio*, the polishing, form-giving stage of poetic composition, is based on the view of art as control and domination of experience relived through memory. Through his example this discovery became an implicit lesson of "literature" in the highest sense to countless generations, as the method of moral self-knowledge and self-improvement, the key to Christian *conversio*, the central and decisive moment in the process of self-analysis which filled all his earthly existence. The *perlegeram* gives the literary basis of this process. Since memory is not passive but creative, we have in Petrarch's method of literary composition a signal confirmation of Roy Pascal's main definition of autobiography as "design," that is, the imposition of a pattern on the past seen from a specific point of view in time, the point of writing, so that an open and possibly chaotic or even absurd chain of life experiences is endowed with a linear, progressive meaning, and a string of perceptions becomes a story, the story of a life.

In the wake of Petrarch, Renaissance Italy produced an unprecedented variety of autobiographical works, in some of which the human psyche was finely and deeply analysed. Between Petrarch and Montaigne at least two other autobiographies deserve our attention, namely those of Leon Battista Alberti (probably written in 1438) and Benvenuto Cellini (written between 1558 and 1568). Alberti's *Vita* takes us with a quantum leap into the middle of the first century of Italian humanism, with the portrait of a cultural hero which immediately strikes us for its contrast with the Petrarchan image. Alberti seems unaffected by the centuries of Christian thought that preceded him. His stated (and achieved) goal is to excel in the pursuit of all the sciences, the arts and letters: in other words, "everything pertaining to fame." This goal is none other than that of the Renaissance *homo universalis*, and in order to achieve it, he spared no effort and applied no moderation. He went well beyond Petrarch's broad yet well-defined fields of endeavour, since he also applied himself to mathematics and the physical sciences, as well as to law and all the practical crafts in which he was able to obtain instruction. Alberti needed no reference to the role of the Divinity so significant in the lives of both Petrarch and Cellini. We know Alberti as a great writer, architect and scientist. His self-portrait offers us even more: an unattainable model of excellence and perfection.

Some one hundred and twenty years later, Cellini started to dictate the story of his life, with the purpose of leaving to posterity a testimony of the struggle of genius against a hostile destiny. Northrop Frye has spoken of the main current of autobiography from Augustine to Rousseau as confession-form. Into that tradition Cellini fits only uneasily, since he seems to have in common with Alberti a lack of need to confess, to lay bare the inner secrets of his soul; he does not see his sins as such. His manner of narrating corresponds rather to that of humanistic historiography, which described events naturalistically as the result of natural forces operating in man. Cellini presents himself as the heroic artistic individual who towers above a society of mediocre and envious rivals or indifferent bystanders. Yet his triumph, despite willpower worthy of an Alberti, is not only impeded at every step by lack of understanding and hostility, but eventually thwarted. Cellini's proud consciousness of his "virtue," in conflict with fate, is the unifying theme of his *Vita*. He never repents or undergoes a conversion; his notion of *virtù* excludes morality, and adds a secular and technical dimension to a word previously charged with religious overtones. Cellini's *virtù* is a Renaissance quality in the narrow sense. He moves with the amorality and immorality of an Achilles who has the right to kill his enemies simply because he is stronger and they are his enemies. The tradition into which Cellini fits is not that of St Augustine or Petrarch but of Plutarch. Cellini represents a new man, centrifugal but problematical. He creates a new genre to express a new man who does not fit into the traditional mould. What is new is the element of the *picaro*, combined with the hero and almost mystic saint, in a unity that was hitherto inconceivable. Cellini foreshadows future times when a man's life will be narrated in order to discover not what is generic but what is characteristic and unique.

Alberti and Cellini provide a bridge between Petrarch, the last Augustinian Christian autobiographer, and Montaigne, the master of modern secular autobiography. Moreover, the French psychological novel of the seventeenth and eighteenth centuries owes no more to French medieval romance than to the almost equally distant, yet equally cogent (although foreign) model of Petrarch, precisely for the extent to which he was responsible for introducing introspection as the very centre of cultural and literary activity. The impact of Petrarch should be combined, as far as France is concerned, with the different (although in our sense convergent) influence of Montaigne.

VICTORIA KAHN

The Figure of the Reader
in Petrarch's Secretum

*Rara lectio est que periculo vacet, nisi legenti lux divine veritatis
affulserit, quid sequendum declinandum ve sit docens.*

(Reading rarely avoids danger, unless the light of divine truth
shines upon the reader, teaching what to seek and what to avoid.)
—*Familiares* 2.8.822

*Nam in omni sermone, gravi presertim et ambiguo, non tam quid
dicatur, quam quid non dicatur attendum est.*

(For in all speech, especially when the matter is serious and
ambiguous, one should pay much less attention to what is said
than to what is not said.)
—*Secretum* 190

A number of critics have recently argued that the aim of literary studies
should be not the interpretation of individual texts but the study of the
conventions of interpretation, and thus of the production and reception of
texts, in different historical periods. Scholars in the field of Renaissance
studies have accordingly made renewed attempts to characterize the changing role of the reader from the early Italian to the later Northern Renaissance. Both Terence Cave and Cathleen Bauschatz have suggested that the
active role of the reader is only recognized in the sixteenth century. Before
that time, the text itself is seen to be authoritative and the reader the
passive recipient of its meaning. Whether this reception is governed by a
patristic, Augustinian notion of allegory or by a conservative Ciceronianism,

From *PMLA* 100, no. 2 (March 1985). © 1985 by the Modern Language Association of America.

the imperative is the disappearance of the reader as a "willful, independent subject." In Augustinian terms, the problematic act of reading is replaced by an "epiphany of grace": "*caritas* equals *claritas.*"

With Erasmus, Rabelais, and Montaigne, on the other hand, an active rhetoric of quotation is said to emerge from the earlier passive or submissive practice of imitation. The literary text is no longer the privileged authority but, rather, something to be dismantled or plundered by would-be authors who, in critically appropriating other texts, redefine the roles of the eventual readers of their own. The redefinition is apparent not least of all, according to Cave, in the fact that "the *figure* of the reader emerges in textual practice." In other words, the reader in the act of making sense is a theme of sixteenth-century texts in a way that is not true of earlier works.

The first problem with this "history" is that it ignores the programmatic statements and rhetorical practice of the early quattrocento humanists who were concerned about defining reading not simply as an act of allegorical or Ciceronian appropriation but as the productive, practical exercise of the reader's judgment. In fact, it was because these authors recognized the potential arbitrariness of interpretation that they wanted to engage and thereby actively educate the reader. Furthermore, this process of education was seen to be not only compatible with but actually dependent on the rhetoric of quotation (i.e., the willful manipulation of prior texts) that Cave and others find characteristic of sixteenth-century works. What is new in the sixteenth century is not the stress on the activity of reading but the refusal, by some authors, to make moral and pedagogical claims for that activity. Yet ambivalence about these claims, an ambivalence embodied in the literary representation of the reader, is apparent in many works of the early Renaissance.

This ambivalence leads us to the second problem with Cave's and Bauschatz's histories. While the suppression of the act of reading may be the ideal in some texts of the earlier Renaissance, there are so many exceptions—so many ironic commentaries on this hermeneutic utopia— that the argument soon loses all heuristic value. As the epigraph from the *Familiares* illustrates, Petrarch in particular was aware of reading as a dangerous activity, one that could only succeed if guided by divine truth, that is, Christian doctrine or the rule of faith. But while true independence of God is theologically impossible, the Petrarchan reader—contrary to the implications of Cave's and Bauschatz's histories—does not simply abdicate all responsibility for judgment. Rather, for Petrarch, as for the quattrocento humanists, divine truth is the condition of interpretive responsibility, of the active exercise of judgment, of the use rather than the abuse of the text. The stress Petrarch's *Secretum* places on the role of the reader illustrates these claims and allows us to begin to revise Cave's and Bauschatz's arguments about conventions of reading in the early Renaissance. This view of Petrarch will also, I hope, help us to see that the interpretation of individual texts is not incompatible with but, rather, inseparable from an investigation into the different conventions of reading prevailing at a given historical moment.

I

The title *Secretum* indicates that the work is primarily a *reading* of Augustine's *Confessions*. As David Marsh has noted, Augustine uses the word "secretum" in book 8 of the *Confessions* to refer to his retreat into the garden where his conversion eventually occurs. It is fitting, then, that the most striking act of interpretation in the *Secretum* (although it is not always recognized for the intentional reading it is) should be Augustinus's account of his conversion.

In the *Confessions* the moment of conversion occurs when Augustine, hearing a voice saying "tolle, lege," picks up the Bible and reads a passage that he applies instantly to himself. This moment of recognition seems to involve no judgment, no reflection. Rather, Augustine is the ideally passive reader Cave describes; the act of reading is eclipsed by the "epiphany of grace." In the *Secretum,* however, Augustinus omits any mention of this scene of reading and stresses instead the willfulness of his conversion. Describing his spiritual conflict in the garden, he writes:

> Et tamen hec inter idem ille qui fueram mansi, donec alta tandem meditatio omnem miseriam meam ante oculos congessit. Itaque postquam plene volui, ilicet et potui, miraque et felicissima celeritate transformatus sum in alterum Augustinum, cuius historie seriem, ni fallor, ex *Confessionibus* meis nosti.

> (Yet nevertheless I remained what I was and no other, until a deep meditation at last showed me the root of all my misery and made it plain before my eyes. And then after that I willed fully, and in that same moment I was able, and by marvelous and blessed alteration I was transformed instantly and made another Augustine altogether. The full history of that transformation is known, if I mistake not, to you already in my *Confessions*.)

Although readers of the *Secretum* have noticed this passage, they have
not remarked on the absence of the original Augustinian scene of reading.
Most have focused on Augustinus's failure to mention the "epiphany of
grace" that is the condition of right reading; as a result they have interpreted
his account ideologically as Petrarch's Stoic or classicizing misreading
of the *Confessions*. This interpretation in turn has led to a variety of
interpretations centering on the existence or nonexistence of ideological
conflict in the dialogue. The question then is whether the two characters
represent separate ideological positions—a medieval insistence on the authority of Christian doctrine versus a nascent humanist insistence on the
authority of personal experience, or the moral rigor of Stoicism versus a
Christian recognition of the divided will. This formulation allows only two
solutions, two interpretations of the text. Franciscus and Augustinus are
either in conflict or in agreement, though this agreement does not imply
Franciscus's ability to act in conformity with his own intellectual grasp of
the truth.

Critical focus on the theme of ideological conflict has diverted attention from the formal and intertextual dimension of the *Secretum* and thus
from those aspects of the text that convey such conflict by raising questions about the act of reading. The central concern of the text is not the
religious issue of Franciscus's sinfulness or the psychological dilemma of
his divided will but rather the problem of defining the will itself as a
faculty of interpretation. Two points should be noted. First, in omitting
the scene of divinely informed reading, Augustinus actually foregrounds
his own and the reader's activity of judgment and interpretation. Second,
this emphasis on judgment compels us to pay attention to the complicated
intertextuality of Augustinus's conversion, and in particular to its relation
to Petrarch's earlier variation on Augustine's *Confessions*, the narration of
his ascent of Mont Ventoux in *Familiares* 4.1. In this well-known letter,
the scene of reading—the potential moment of conversion—is all-important,
and Petrarch's failure to become an "alter Franciscus" is the more striking
for his deliberate allusion to Augustine's sudden transformation. But, as a
close reading of this letter also reveals, Petrarch is primarily concerned not
with whatever divine intervention may have occurred at the moment of
Augustine's reading but with the unified will that is the precondition of his
reading. Thus the seemingly antithetical accounts function in similar ways,
both serving to characterize the Petrarchan persona not as the ideally
passive reader but rather as the willful (mis)reader who fails to imitate his
master. What I am suggesting, in short, is that Augustinus's emphasis on
the role of the will in his conversion seems less curious, less simply

erroneous, once we see that the *Secretum*, like the "Ascent," takes as its subject such willful (mis)reading, that it, in fact, describes all reading as a correct or incorrect disposition of the will.

Existential problems are clearly inseparable from interpretive problems in this dialogue; as Franciscus remarks in book 3, his past experience is a book like his other books ("experientie liber"), none of which, according to Augustinus, he knows how to read. But the important point for our purposes is that the Augustinian theme of the divided will in the *Secretum* both converges with and mirrors a conflict of interpretations or of intertextual alliances: on the one hand, Augustine's reading of his own experience in the *Confessions* and, on the other, Petrarch's prior reading of the *Confessions* in the "Ascent of Mont Ventoux"; one, an exemplary narrative of conversion, the other a letter that complicates the possibility of imitating such an example. An intertextual reading of Petrarch's text, then, suggests that what is at issue in the dialogue is not only the status of the divided will that keeps Franciscus from conforming to the Augustinian ideology of reading but the coherence of that ideology itself.

This ideology, the following pages make clear, is based in part on a Platonic theory of reminiscence. To be cured of his spiritual sickness, Franciscus has only to remember the truth of any text he reads (for a Christian reader, it is always the same truth) and will to conform to it. But if, as Augustinus gradually acknowledges, remembering or reading correctly is itself an act of the will, then the individual who does not have the will to conform will not have the ability to remember either. As Augustinus remarks of Franciscus's love of Laura in book 3, "verum est, cum in aliis tum in hac precipue passione, quod unus quisque suarum rerum est benignus interpres (It is true, in particular in this passion, as in all others, each is a benign interpreter of his own affairs)."

The problem under discussion in the dialogue, then, is not simply Franciscus's psychological resistance but also the resistance of all texts to yield up their secrets—as if the real meaning were something that one could locate just beneath the surface of the apparent meaning and then record in memory or in notes. The psychological dilemma is finally an interpreter's dilemma, one that becomes even more striking when we see that the poet's desire for Laura is glossed as a will to interpretation.

II

To understand the "Augustinian" ideology of reading, we need to consider how Petrarch sees the narrative of the *Confessions*. In the *Secre-*

tum, as in the "Ascent," the converted Augustine stands for the possibility of a certain kind of interpretation and thus of a certain kind of recounting of experience—an interpretation that can take the form of a coherent narration ("historié seriem [linear history]") because, from the perspective of conversion, events are seen to be informed by divine intention. Significantly, at the beginning of book 10 of the *Confessions*—the first book after the narrative proper that might be said to examine the conditions of the possibility of the previous autobiography—Augustine discusses memory, distinguishing between memory as a place and memory as a divinely informed activity (see 10.8). It is the latter, converted memory that collects and orders the fragments of past experience into a coherent self, that is, a coherent narrative. The association of coherent self and narrative is apparent early in book 2, in a passage that Petrarch refers to in the "Ascent." Augustine writes:

> Recordari volo transactas foeditates meas, et carnales corruptiones animae meae, non quod eas amem, sed ut amem te, deus meus. Amore amoris tui facio istuc, recolens vias meas nequissimas in amaritudine recogitationis meae, ut tu dulcescas mihi, dulcedo non fallax, dulcedo felix et secura, et colligens me a dispersione, in qua frustatim discissus sum, dum ab uno te aversus in multa evanui.

> (I will now call to mind my over-passed impurities, and the fleshly corruptions of my soul: not because I love them, but that I may love thee, O my God. For love of thy love I do it; in the very bitterness of my remembrance repeating over my most wicked courses, that thou mayest only grow sweet unto me; (thou Sweetness never beguiling, thou happy and secure Sweetness!) and recollecting myself out of that broken condition of mine, wherein I was piecemeal shattered asunder; while being turned away from thee alone, I squandered myself upon many vanities.)

(2.1)

Petrarch, recalling this passage on the top of Mont Ventoux, reflects:

> Tempus forsan veniet, quando eodem quo gesta sunt ordine universa percurram, prefatus illud Augustini tui: "Recordari."

> (The time perhaps will come when I will run through all things in the order in which they were done, prefacing them with that remark of your Augustine, "I will now call to mind.")

"Colligens me a dispersione" in Augustine's address to God should be understood almost as a kind of creation ex nihilo: the self ("me") is only truly constituted by the orderly ("ordine" in Petrarch's account) act of narration, or, rather, the self and the orderly narration are produced at the same time. But the constitution of the self is also the surrender of the self to God; the desire for confession is a desire for an object beyond oneself. Because self-knowledge is ultimately knowledge of God's Word, scriptural exegesis finally replaces autobiography in the *Confessions*.

Karlheinz Stierle's work on exemplary narrative can further help us to characterize Augustine's narrative. In narratives intended to be exemplary, like the converted Augustine's, history or narrative

> se constitue d'un point de vue philosophico-moral. Elle apparaît comme détachée de continuum historique et contient son sens en elle-même. Elle est un macro-exemple. Les critères qui president à la traduction de l'événement en histoire sont ceux de la philosophie morale [or Christian doctrine], qui s'impriment dans l'ensemble mémorable d'une histoire. Ce qui s'accomplit lors de la traduction d'un événement en histoire se répète lors de la traduction de l'histoire en exemples.

> (is constituted from a philosophico-moral point of view. It appears as though detached from a historical continuum and contains its meaning within itself. It is a macro-example. The criteria that preside over the translation of the event into history are those of moral philosophy [or Christian doctrine], which inscribes itself in the memorable whole of a history. What is achieved when an event is translated into history is repeated in the translation of history into examples.)

In this view of narration as teleological and closed, the privileged position of the narrator is simply the reverse side of the moral exemplarity of the account. The further assumption is that the exempla within the text have universal implications; they are intended to be imitated, their aim is persuasion to moral action.

Petrarch shares this concept of history as example. In the preface to his *De viris illustribus*, he presents isolated moral examples rather than an extended narrative, but these examples (or brief narratives) are ideally seen as the conditions of the possibility of the right kind of history. He first describes his work in a way that recalls Augustine's discussion of the place of memory in book 10 of the *Confessions*, and he thereby suggests that

De viris serves as a kind of artificial memory, a "commemoratio virtutum."
But he goes on to argue that what remained "sparsa" and "disseminata"
in the texts of others has been not only collected ("collecta") in his text
but ordered and composed. Just as in classical rhetoric invention must be
followed by disposition, so the effectiveness or usefulness of the *place* of
memory depends on the constructive *activity* of memory. Unlike those
historians who cite differing authorities "so that the entire text of their
history is lost in cloudy ambiguities and inexplicable conflicts," Petrarch
claims to have composed a unified whole ("unam feci"). Finally, Petrarch
articulates Stierle's claim that the wholeness and linearity of the narrative—
its refusal of digression—are tied up with its moral exemplariness:

> Hic enim, nisi fallor, fructuosus historici finis est, illa prosequi
> que vel sectanda legentibus vel fugienda sunt, ut in utranque
> partem copia suppetat illustrium exemplorum. Quisquis extra
> hos terminos evagari presumpserit, sciat se alienam aream terere,
> alienis finibus errare, memineritque e vestigio redeundum nisi
> forte oblectandi gratia diversoria legentibus interdum grata
> quesierit.

> (This is the profitable goal of the historian: to point up to the
> readers those things that are to be followed and those to be
> avoided, with plenty of distinguished examples provided on
> either side. Whatever author would presume to wander outside
> this boundary, let him know that he is treading on foreign soil
> and wandering in foreign territory, and let him be reminded to
> return to the beaten path, except perhaps when he will be
> seeking, at a certain point, to please the readers with amusing
> anecdotes.)

> *(De viris illustribus)*

Digression is permissible for the sake of amusement, but it should always
be subordinate to the purposes of moral instruction. Thus, while certain
anecdotes are permissible, those that are merely digressive are not. As in
the passage I quoted earlier from the *Confessions*, the pleasure we take in
digression should be a "dulcedo non fallax (sweetness never beguiling)."
The moral criteria of selection, then, dictate the exclusion of certain
irrelevant examples, examples that cannot be usefully subsumed under a
general rule:

> Nec vero me tanta in re segnem atque attenuatam operam
> consumpsisse profitebor, ut et prodessem simul ac placerem,

multa resecantem que plus confusionis ut dixi supra quam commoditatis allatura videbantur et brevitati consulentem pariter et notitie rerum memorandarum. Quid enim, ne res exemplo careat, quid nosse attinet quos servos aut canes vir illustris habuerit, que iumenta, quas penulas, que servorum nomina, quod coniugium artificium peculium ve, quibus cibis uti solitus, quo vehiculo, quibus phaleris, quo amictu, quo denique salsamento, quo genere leguminis delectatus sit?

(In a work of this size, I have expended long and painstaking labor in order that I might be both useful and pleasing. I have omitted many things which, as I said above, seemed to lend more to confusion than to usefulness, while I have striven at the same time for brevity and for a description of the really important events. For what use is it, to give some examples, to know what slaves or dogs an illustrious man has had, what beasts of burden, what cloaks, what were the names of his servants, what was the nature of his married life, his professions, or his personal property? What use is it to know what sort of food he liked best, or what he preferred as a means of transportation, as a breastplate, as a cloak, or finally, even for sauces and vegetables?)

The preface to *De viris* stresses the role of the author, suggesting that the reader's is relatively unproblematic. But, as we will see, Franciscus in the *Secretum* is first of all a reader, and he raises questions, both in his direct discourse and in his practice of citation, about the reader who, like the author Petrarch censures, wanders outside the boundaries of permissible (i.e., ethical) interpretation. Thus, for example, in response to Augustinus's account of his conversion, Franciscus remarks that in reading the *Confessions* he seems to read his own story; but for Augustinus's "historie seriem" he substitutes "mee peregrinationis historiam (my story of peregrination)." The substitution is not innocent; it marks Franciscus's ability to identify with Augustine's wandering, his error, but not with his exemplary conversion. In short, Franciscus sees the *Confessions* as foreign soil or foreign territory, and it is only with Augustine's account of alienation, not with the orderliness of its recapitulation in memory, that Franciscus the exile feels at home.

Memory as the condition of self-knowledge and right action is a problem from the very beginning of the *Secretum*, as we see by Augustinus's first words, which depict Franciscus as self-forgetful: "miseriarum ne tuarum sic prorsus oblitus es? An non te mortalem esse meministi? (Have you so entirely forgotten your miseries? Don't you remember that you are mortal?)." In fact, the whole of the *Secretum* might be seen as Augustinus's attempt to get Franciscus to remember himself (his sins and the possibility of salvation) and to forget others (Laura and the reading public). In book 1 Augustinus associates memory with reading when he argues that reading correctly means "to commit to memory (memorie commendare)." (And further on Franciscus characterizes writing as memory when he remarks that Augustinus has recorded ("praeclarissime meministi") the sickness of the imagination in his *De vera religione*. But Franciscus's characterization of his own reading of this text begins to raise the questions inherent in the association of right reading with memory that Augustinus and Franciscus will confront over and over again:

> In quem librum [*De vera religione*] nuper incidi, a philosophorum et poetarum lectione digrediens, itaque cupidissime perlegi: haud aliter quam qui videndi studio peregrinatur a patria, ubi ignotum famose cuiuspiam urbis limen ingreditur, nova captus locorum dulcedine passimque subsistens, obvia queque circumspicit.

> (I recently came upon this book, leaving behind my reading of philosophers and poets, and thus read it most avidly: like one who has traveled abroad out of the desire of seeing new sights, and who crosses the unknown threshold of a famous city, and captured by the sweetness of these new places, stops here and there and observes closely everything he encounters.)

It is characteristic of Petrarch to describe his encounter with an authoritative precursor as an encounter with an alien other, but his use of the term "peregrinatio" here, as well as "captus locorum dulcedine," suggests that his reading of *De vera religione*, like his reading of the *Confessions* and, as we will see, of his own *Secretum*, fails to have the moral effect that Augustinus associates with right reading. Thus while Augustinus first seems to suggest that Franciscus's spiritual problem is only forgetfulness, the dialogue gradually elaborates a more complicated view of Franciscus's condition. Memory is just the first step. One must then be able to apply what one remembers from reading, and this necessity in turn raises the question of the *way* in which one applies it, that is, of the criterion of application. This criterion, to come full circle, is also the standard by which one judges what one reads.

I do not mean to suggest that the *Secretum* proceeds as a coherent argument about the conditions of the possibility of right interpretation. To the contrary, while the dialogue gradually moves from problems of reading to problems of writing, the relation of memory to the act of reading and to action in general is not resolved once and for all but replayed in a variety of exchanges—exchanges that complicate rather than illustrate the concept of the moral exemplarity of the text. A close look at two passages in book 2 of the *Secretum* illustrates this point, for they raise questions regarding Augustinus's optimism about his effectiveness and about the *possibility* of his role as a Platonic midwife who simply reminds his charge of what he has forgotten.

III

The problem of reading exemplary texts is taken up at one point in book 2 when Franciscus complains about the distractions of city life. Augustinus reminds him of Seneca's arguments in *De tranquillitate animi*; Franciscus replies that while he is reading this text it is helpful but that "libro autem e manibus elapso assensio simul omnis intercidit (no sooner is the book from my hands than all my feeling for it vanishes)." Augustinus responds that Franciscus does not know *how* to read. Yet while Augustinus associates memory with the right application of the text, his wording begins to suggest the inadequacy of his advice:

> Quotiens legenti salutares se se offerunt sententie, quibus vel excitari sentis animum vel frenari, noli viribus ingenii fidere, sed illas in memorie penetralibus absconde multoque studio tibi familiares effice; ut, quod experti solent medici, quocunque loco vel tempore dilationis impatiens morbus invaserit, habeas velut in animo conscripta remedia.

> (Whenever you read a book and meet with any wholesome maxims by which you feel your spirit stirred or enthralled, do not trust merely to the resources of your wits, but make a point of learning them by heart and making them quite familiar by meditating on them, as doctors do with their experiments, so that no matter when or where some urgent case of illness arises, you have the remedy written, so to speak, in your head.)
>
> (Secretum)

In the traditional view, as we have seen, exempla provide the reader with a cultural, artificial memory, a Ciceronian storehouse of common-

places that can serve the reader as remedies when needed. But the relation
between memory and example is more complicated here. First of all, it is
not enough to read; one must hide what one reads in the memory, write it
on the mind. Further on, however, the metaphor of writing is literalized,
when Augustinus advises Franciscus to mark *in the text* those passages
containing useful moral sententiae. Here the text is not simply preserved in
the memory, memory itself is preserved in the text. But if memory needs
the external aid of writing, the problem of applying one's reading is not
resolved; it is merely reduplicated in the artificial memory of notes. To
hide something in one's memory, then, is indeed to put it out of sight, as
the ambiguous "absconde" suggests. The secrets of the text, a secular
version of what Augustine calls "tot paginarum opaca secreta (so many
pages full of dark secrets)" (*Confessions* 11.2), are likely to remain secret
even to oneself, for neither the original text nor the notes can guarantee
conversion to action.

This problem of the relation of exemplum to imitation or application
is discussed earlier in book 2, when Augustinus inquires:

> Fidis ingenio et librorum lectione multorum. . . . Lectio autem
> ista quid profuit? . . . Quanquam vel multa nosse quid revelat
> si, cum celi terreque ambitum, si, cum maris spatium et astrorum
> cursus herbarumque virtutes ac lapidum et nature secreta
> didiceritis, vobis estis incogniti? Si, cum rectam virtutis ardue
> semitam scripturis ducibus agnoveritis, obliquo calle transversos
> agit furor.

> (You trust in your intellect and in your having read many
> books. . . . But what has that reading profited you? . . . And of
> what relevance is it to know a multitude of things if, when you
> have learned the circuits of the heavens and the earth, the
> spaces of the sea, the courses of the stars, the virtues of herbs and
> stones, the secrets of nature, you are still ignorant of yourself?
> If by the help of Scripture you shall have discovered the right
> and upward path, what use is it if wrath and passion make
> you swerve aside into the crooked, downward way.)

Here the same Augustinian passage that Petrarch reads during his ascent of
Mont Ventoux functions to conflate a certain way of reading with the vain
admiration of the external world (paradoxically described as "secreta").
Reading can distract us from the self just as much as nature can, if the
pleasure we take in discourse ("voluptatem ex sermone") is divorced from

moral considerations ("sua probra"; cf. *Confessions* 1.13). Furthermore, the play on the word *secret* calls attention to the ambivalent function of Petrarch's allusion to the *Confessions*. The Augustinian passage, which occurs during the discussion of memory in book 10, argues that natural wonders are nothing compared with the wonder of human memory. In the *Secretum*, however, the text—which ideally helps to preserve memory—is stigmatized as a means to self-forgetfulness, and reading is seen as insepa-rable from the "concupiscentia oculorum (concupiscence of the eyes)" that Augustine condemns in the *Confessions*. Not only do one's nonliterary passions obstruct the application of the text, the text itself can become an object of desire.

One of the many ways in which the *Secretum* indicates this desire is in the two interlocutors' use and abuse of the work of others. Throughout the dialogue Franciscus and Augustinus have been reading other texts implicitly, as their practice of citation shows, but at one crucial moment in book 2 they explicitly address the issue of the use of texts, when Franciscus offers two allegorical interpretations of a passage from Virgil (*Aeneid* 1.52–57). Augustinus responds:

> Sive enim id Virgilius ipse sensit, dum scriberet, sive ab omni tali consideratione remotissimus . . . hoc tamen, quod de irarum impetu et rationis imperio dixisti, facete satis et proprie dictum puto.

> (For whether Vergil had this in mind when writing, or whether [he was] without any such idea . . . what you have said about the rush of anger and the authority of reason seems to me expressed with equal wit and truth.)

This exchange suggests that an author's intention, even when recoverable, is not the criterion of interpretation; instead, the virtue of any particular reading must be judged by its conformity to Christian doctrine. In book 2 this issue of the use of citations, and thus of the way in which one applies one's reading, is foregrounded in the specific conflict of interpretations regarding a passage from Cicero's *De senectute*: "Si in hoc erro, libenter erro, neque hunc errorem auferri michi volo, dum vivo (If I err I err here willingly, and I shall never consent to part with this error as long as I live)." When Franciscus quotes these lines to defend his love of Laura, Augustinus objects that the subject of the passage is immortality, not profane love. Yet, while Augustinus does invoke Cicero's intention to support this objection, the real criterion, he goes on to suggest, is not intention but moral effect: "tu in opinione fedissima atque falsissima iisdem verbis abuteris (You, however, to urge the ignoblest and most false of all opinions, abuse those same terms)." At issue here is the intrinsic moral status of the example. In the preface to *De viris*, Petrarch argues that certain examples are morally instructive and that noninstructive ones must be excluded from the text of history. Yet in book 3 of the *Secretum*, the example has clearly lost its absolute moral authority and serves to illustrate only the possible conflict of interpretations. I cite just one instance: when Augustinus tendentiously inquires whether Franciscus has looked in the mirror lately, whether he has noticed his gray hair, we are supposed to understand the underlying *contemptus mundi* argument. But Franciscus only responds by citing a number of classical examples of men who were prematurely gray. In so doing, he introduces precisely the sort of example that Petrarch the historian censures. Augustinus then comments that Franciscus's use of examples has become divorced from their correct moral application, and, at the same time, he puns on Petrarch's earlier work:

> Ingens tibi exemplorum copia est; tanta utinam eorum, que cogitationem mortis ingererent. . . . Tu vero, cum ad canitiem iubeo respicere, canorum illustrium virorum turbam profers.

> (What vast abundance of examples you can command! Pray heaven you have as many recollections of your own death. . . . When I bid you think on your own whitening forehead, you quote me a crowd of famous men whose locks were white also.)

In this view all interpretation is arbitrary in relation to the text but not in relation to the text's use, that is, to morality. Thus, a little earlier, when Augustinus cites two lines from Homer to describe Franciscus's condition as a solitary lover, he claims not that Homer intended such an application of the lines, only that such an application is possible ("dici posset"). And, as Augustinus reminds us elsewhere, "posse (to be able)" and "velle (to will)" are the same thing. The implication is that every interpretation, morally sound or not, is a function of the will. (Augustinus, as we have seen, comments on the negative instance of such interpretation when he remarks of Franciscus's love, "it is true, in this particular passion, as in all others, each is a benign interpreter of his own affairs." If, however, will or desire rather than memory guides our reading and our actions, the suggestion is not just that reading educates the will but also that the divinely informed will is the condition of right reading, a problem that Franciscus explicitly addresses toward the end of the dialogue.)

This stress on the willfulness or eroticism of interpretation may explain why Augustinus compares Franciscus separated from Laura to Orpheus *united with* Eurydice and why Franciscus first greets the as-yet-unnamed figure of "Veritas" in the proem of the *Secretum* with the words that Aeneas addresses to Venus. It also explains, I think, why Augustinus consistently compares Franciscus's efforts to attain self-knowledge to the struggles of the Virgilian hero (Aeneas or another). For example, when in book 1 Augustinus urges Franciscus to leave the wide path of the "vulgus" for the narrow way of spiritual struggle, he cites Apollo's address to Ascanius in book 9 of the *Aeneid* (l. 641): "macte nova virtute, puer: sic itur ad astra (A blessing, child, on thy young valour! So man scales the stars)." Even when he is chastising Franciscus for his recalcitrance, he does so in words that suggest the heroism of Franciscus's resistance; in the following citation the lapsed Franciscus becomes the resolute Aeneas (*Aeneid* 4.449): "mens immota manet, lacrimae volvuntur inanes (Steadfast stands his will; the tears fall in vain)." It is only toward the end of book 3, when Augustinus tries to distinguish between the metaphorical vehicle of the Virgilian passages and their Christian application—when he, in other words, wants to caution Franciscus against identifying too strongly with the this-worldly glory that the epic hero attains—that he substitutes quotations from the *Eclogues* and the *Aeneid* on the transience of human life for his earlier descriptions of Aeneas's heroism. It is also at this point that he stresses, in striking contrast to books 1 and 2, the fragility of human memory and human monuments, the inevitable destruction or oblivion of books.

That this caution is necessary is apparent from the very beginning of book 3. If books 1 and 2 raise the problem of the will in relation to right reading and discuss reading itself as evidence of the state of the will, book 3 comments more explicitly on Franciscus's recalcitrance both as a reader and as a lover by tying it to his desire for fame as a writer. Thus, while the book continues Augustinus's arraignment of Franciscus's sins, it is not by chance that "Amor" and "Gloria" have been saved for the last, since together they articulate the relation of Franciscus's psychological conflict to his literary ambition and the displacement of the former by the latter. Laura is both the object of desire and the means to poetic glory, but poetic glory is also, for Franciscus, an object of desire in its own right. The temptation is for Laura to be displaced by the desire for writing. Just as memory is replaced by writing in book 2, so, paradoxically, is Laura forgotten as Franciscus commemorates her name in his poetry:

Quis digne satis execretur aut stupeat hanc alienate mentis insaniam cum, non minus nominis quam ipsius corporis splendore captus, quicquid illi consonum fuit incredibili vanitate coluisti? Quam ob causam tanto opere sive cesaream sive poeticam lauream, quod illa hoc nomine vocaretur, adamasti; ex eoque tempore sine lauri mentione vix ullum tibi carmen effluxit, non aliter quam si vel Penei gurgitis accola vel Cirrei verticis sacerdos existeres. Denique quia cesaream sperare fas non erat, lauream poeticam, quam studiorum tuorum tibi meritum promittebat, nichilo modestius quam dominam ipsam adamaveras concupisti.

(Who could sufficiently utter his indignation and amazement at this sign of a distempered mind, that, infatuated as much by the beauty of her name as of her person, you have with perfectly incredible silliness paid honour to anything that has the remotest connection with that name itself? Had you any liking for the laurel of empire or of poetry, it was because the name they bore was hers; and from this time onwards there is hardly a verse from your pen but in it you have made mention of the laurel, as if indeed you were a denizen of Peneus' stream, or some priest of Cirrha's mount. And finally, discovering that the laurel of empire was beyond your reach, you have, with as little self-restraint as you showed in the case of your beloved herself, now coveted the laurel of Poetry of which the merit of your words seemed to give more promise.)

That Laura is indeed forgotten is reflected in the progression of book 3 itself, in which the discussion of Laura gives way to a discussion of Petrarch's literary production. Whereas book 2 presents reading as a form of self-forgetfulness and writing as a kind of artificial memory, here writing (the poet's desire) becomes (like the lover's desire) a way of losing oneself. Augustinus uses passages from Petrarch's *Africa* to argue against Franciscus, thereby illustrating that as an author Franciscus wrote for others, not for himself, and that as a reader he was incapable of using his text (or any other) to his own advantage. In other words, once the analogy between desire and writing is spelled out, as it is in the passage quoted above, the debate about the right way to cure Franciscus of his love can be applied to his sickness as a reader as well.

The problem is that to use the text correctly, one already has to have the rectified will that the text is supposed to educate, just as in order to flee Laura, Franciscus must have the resolution that he can only acquire by having already fled (actually or emotionally). Franciscus is like the youth who complains of having learned nothing from traveling and to whom Socrates replies, "Tecum enim ... peregrinabaris (You voyage with yourself)." To Augustinus's advice to flee Laura, Franciscus responds:

> Miro modo perplexus sum. Tu enim, dum michi curandi sanandique animi documenta prebes, curandum prius sanandumque predicas, ac demum fugiendum. Atqui de hoc ipso dubitatur, qualiter sit curandus. Si enim curatus est, quid ultra queritur? Si autem incuratus, ubi locorum mutatio (quod tu ipse astruis) non adiuvat.

> (I must say I am perplexed. You give me a prescription to cure and heal my soul and tell me I must first heal it and then flee. Now, my difficulty is I do not know how to heal it. If it is cured, what more do I need? But if, again, it is not cured, what good will change of scene bring me?)

Like the optimistic interpreter who presupposes a benign rather than a vicious hermeneutic circle, Augustinus argues for the possibility of preparing the reader or lover, of gradually educating the will, but, as we will see, Franciscus and Petrarch both remain recalcitrant.

In the conclusion of the *Secretum* Franciscus recalls Augustine's discussion of memory in the *Confessions*, as well as his own in *De viris illustribus*, but only to signal his failure "to compose a unified text (unam facere)." He is still divided, still dispersed and fragmented. His condition reflects his persistent concern with human glory—in other words, with the form of speech that Augustinus defines as "vulgar and scattered (vulgatum ac sparsum)." He is only in part different from what he was when the conversation began. And this incomplete transformation recalls both the first poem of the *Canzoniere* and the conclusion to the "Ascent of Mont Ventoux." In all three works the moment of conversion is deferred by the act of writing itself. In the "Ascent," Petrarch tells us that he hurried down the mountain to the inn because he was afraid that if he delayed, his feelings would change and he would lose his desire—not the desire to act according to his newfound insight but the desire to write an account of his experience. He ends by asking his correspondent, Dionigi, to pray that he will be converted some day, but it is clear from the final Virgilian allusion, "per multa iactati (much tossed about)," that the representation of his heroic "peregrinationes" is his immediate concern. The final lines of the *Secretum* echo the conclusion of the "Ascent," though this time both roles are taken by Franciscus. He prays for himself, but the moment of self-identity is deferred, the present task of writing insisted on:

> Adero michi ipse quantum potero, et sparsa anime fragmenta recolligam, moraborque mecum sedulo. Sane nunc, dum loquimur, multa me magnaque, quamvis adhuc mortalia, negotia expectant.

> (I will be present to myself, as far as I am able. I will collect the scattered fragments of my soul, and will make a great endeavor to possess myself in patience. But even while we speak, a crowd of important affairs, though only of the world, is waiting for my attention.)

As in the *Canzoniere*, to collect the "sparsa anime fragmenta"—the Augustinian formulation for remembering oneself—is to silence the "sermonem vulgatum et sparsum" of the reading public, of fame. Forgetfulness of oneself, peregrination, is thus a condition of writing the *Secretum*—a work that, like the "Ascent," follows on and replaces a potential conversion.

This incomplete transformation, which Augustinus calls a "relapse" ("in antiquam litem relabimur (We are falling into our old controversy)," sheds some light on Petrarch's characterization of the *Secretum* in the proem to the dialogue:

> Hoc igitur tam familiare colloquium ne forte dilaberetur, dum scriptis mandare instituo, mensuram libelli huius implevi. Non quem annumerari aliis operibus meis velim, aut unde gloriam petam (maiora quedam mens agitat) sed ut dulcedinem, quam semel ex collocutione percepi, quotiens libuerit ex lectione percipiam.

> (That this discourse, so intimate and deep, might not be lost, I have set it down in writing and made this book; not that I wish to class it with my other works, or desire for it any credit. My thoughts aim higher. What I desire is that I may be able by reading to renew as often as I wish the pleasure I felt from the discourse itself.)

Here memory has indeed been externalized and reading has become an iterative act that provides the reader not with moral exempla but with aesthetic pleasure—the pleasure we take in the textual imitation rather than in (our) imitating that representation. The text has in short become the "spectaculum" and the reader the spectator of the troubles or sufferings represented. As Augustinus argues in book 2, this theatrical view of, or aesthetic distance from, experience can lead to a Stoic acceptance of suffering; but the danger is also (as all critics of the theater have recognized) that the spectator will be hardened to the represented experience, a moral danger that is even greater when the represented individual is oneself.

There is a further problem with the characterization of the *Secretum* as a kind of artificial memory that will enable Petrarch to remember his exchange with Augustinus, for this exchange never, strictly speaking, took place. Of course, one could reply that the fiction of memory is easily grasped, that it has a clear pedagogical function. But even there the word "memory" (like Franciscus's desire) has no single referent. Is it the memory of human fame that Petrarch intends to acquire by means of this dialogue (as the emphasis on the pleasure of reading might suggest), or is it the memory of the vanity of human fame (an interpretation supported by the "nonpublication" of the work)? Is it the memory of Saint Augustine's *Confessions* or the memory of Petrarch's own confessions in the "Ascent"?

The question is even more complicated when we recall that the "Ascent" is itself the site of conflicting imitative allegiances, on the one hand to Livy's account of Hannibal's ascent of Mount Haemus, on the other to Augustine's account of his conversion. If we contend, as Thomas Greene does, that the text dramatizes a conflict between imitative and allegorical ways of reading and writing, then it is clear that Petrarch's partial allegorization of his experience marks the failure of the nascent humanist mode of imitation in this text. But, as Greene is well aware, Augustine's *Confessions* not only represents the possibility of a transcendental or allegorical interpretation of experience but constitutes an object of imitation in itself; it seems clear, then, that Petrarch does not simply fail to imitate in the "Ascent" but quite self-consciously *represents* his failure to imitate as a "perverse and wicked imitation" of Augustine's *Confessions*. Whereas Augustine's narrative in the *Confessions* derives from the unified will that was the precondition of conversion ("plene volui"), Petrarch's narrative dramatizes in its conflicting rhetorical modes the divided will that precludes conversion. The moral problem is an interpretive one, for the will to conversion is at the same time a will to a certain kind of interpretation. Thus the divided will, the source of Petrarch's doubts about the symbolism of his experience on the mountain, is reflected in the division between a consistent allegorical reading of his experience and a critique of the willfulness or hubris of such reading. What Petrarch is in fact reflecting on is the difference between being a character *in* an allegory and being an interpreter *of* allegory, that is to say, an allegorizer. In insisting on his role as interpreter of his experience, he also insists on the failure of his attempt to view that experience as an allegory. Similarly, the *Secretum* does not simply fail to imitate the *Confessions* but insists on that failure as a mode of interpretation. In this light, Greene's remark about the "Ascent"—"the whole experience comes to be *one more example* in an indefinite series"—should be applied to the later text as well: the *Secretum* is an example that raises doubts about the very possibility of the example; it is a dialogue on reading that questions the possibility of reading the dialogue as exemplary.

Finally, insofar as the dialogue does question the possibility of an exemplary reading, it also portrays reading as a problematic *activity* and thus cautions us against seeing this conception as "originating" in the sixteenth century. As I suggested in the beginning of this essay, what is new in this century and with Montaigne in particular is not the questioning of the possibility of the exemplary text but rather the ironic commentary on the desire for such exempla. In Petrarch's *Secretum* this desire is still very real, and it motivates the metadiscursive reflection, the reflection on the use and abuse of the divinely given will to signify.

Chronology

1304	Petrarch born on July 20 at Arezzo.
1309	Clement V moves papal seat to Avignon. Robert "the Wise" becomes King of Naples.
1311	Family at Pisa; meets Dante.
1312	Family settles in Carpentras, after journey through Genoa, Marseilles, and Avignon. Petrarch begins study of *trivium*.
1316	Begins study of law at Montpellier.
1320	Continues legal studies at Bologna.
1321	Death of Dante.
1326	Settles in Avignon following his father's death. Begins ecclesiastical career (he never went further than the minor orders).
1327	During Holy Week Petrarch sees Laura in church of Santa Chiara in Avignon.
1330	In Gascony with Bishop Giacomo Colonna; later returns to Avignon under protection of Cardinal Giovanni Colonna. Composes *Epistolae metricae*.
1333	Travels in France, Germany, and Flanders.
1336	Climbs Mont Ventoux; travels in Italy (first visit to Rome, January 1337), perhaps Spain and England. Birth of his son Giovanni (mother unknown).
1337	Retires to Vaucluse. Boccaccio writes the *Filostrato*. Beginning of the Hundred Years War.
1338	Begins *Africa* and *De viris illustribus*.
1341	Crowned Poet Laureate by Robert of Naples on Capitoline in Rome.
1342	Studies Greek. Begins his *Secretum*.
1343	Becomes papal ambassador at Court of Naples. His illegitimate daughter Francesca born. Death of Robert of Naples, succeeded by Joanna I.

1344	Begins *Liber rerum memorandarum* at Parma.
1345	Escapes from besieged Parma. Attacked by bandits at Reggio. Puts son in school in Verona. Discovers Cicero's letters *Ad atticum*. Returns to Vaucluse.
1346	Begins *De vita solitaria* and *Bucolicum carmen*.
1347	Visits his brother in Charterhouse of Montrieux. Starts for Rome to salute Cola di Rienzi, who has made himself master of the city, but stops at Genoa on learning of Cola's reverses.
1348	The year of the Plague. Death of Laura. Boccaccio begins *The Decameron*.
1349	Prepares first versions of sonnets (*Canzoniere*), starts to collect letters (*Familiares*).
1350	In Verona, Mantua, Rome, and Arezzo. Charles IV imprisons Cola di Rienzi at Prague.
1351	In Padua, where Boccaccio delivers invitation to lecture in Florence. Petrarch refuses, and returns to Vaucluse.
1352	Begins the *Triumphs* (*Trionfi*).
1353	At court of the Visconti in Milan, where he remains eight years.
1354	Final fall of Cola di Rienzi.
1355	Ambassador to Imperial Court at Prague. Writes *Contra medicum quendam*. Appointed Court Palatine. Charles IV crowned Emperor at Rome.
1356	Releases *De vita solitaria* and *De otio religioso*.
1357	Releases *Bucolicum carmen*.
1358	Writes the *Itinerarium syriacum*.
1361	In Paris on political mission. Returns to Milan to escape plague. Moves to Padua, then to Venice, where he is given a palace by the Senate.
1364–65	Arranges his letters (*Familiares*).
1366	Finishes *De remediis utriusque fortunae*.
1367	*De sui ipsius et multorum ignorantia*.
1368	Settles at Arquà with daughter and son-in-law.
1374	Possible meeting with Chaucer in Padua. Petrarch dies at Arquà.
1375	Death of Boccaccio.
1377	Return of papal court to Rome.

Contributors

HAROLD BLOOM, Sterling Professor of the Humanities at Yale University, is the author of *The Anxiety of Influence, Poetry and Repression*, and many other volumes of literary criticism. His forthcoming study, *Freud: Transference and Authority*, attempts a full-scale reading of all of Freud's major writings. A MacArthur Prize Fellow, he is general editor of five series of literary criticism published by Chelsea House. During 1987–88, he served as Charles Eliot Norton Professor of Poetry at Harvard University.

ALDO S. BERNARDO, Professor of Italian at the State University of New York at Binghamton, is the author of *Petrarch, Scipio and the* Africa and *Petrarch, Laura and the* Triumphs, and is the editor of several anthologies, including *Dante, Petrarch and Boccaccio*.

ROBERT M. DURLING, Professor of Italian at the University of California, Santa Cruz, is the translator of Petrarch's *Canzoniere* and the author of *The Figure of the Poet in the Renaissance Epic*.

JOHN FRECCERO is Rosina Pierotti Professor of Italian at Stanford University and is the author of important works on Italian literature. His most recent book is *Dante: The Poetics of Conversion*.

GIUSEPPE MAZZOTTA is Professor of Italian at Yale University. His works include *Dante, Poet of the Desert* and *The World at Play in Boccaccio's* Decameron.

MARGUERITE WALLER teaches English at Amherst College and is the author of *Petrarch's Poetics and Literary History* as well as several articles, including "Poetic Influence in Hollywood."

THOMAS M. GREENE is Frederick Clifford Ford Professor of English and Comparative Literature at Yale. His critical works include *The Descent from Heaven, Rabelais: A Study in Comic Courage, The Light in*

Troy: Imitation and Discovery in Renaissance Poetry, and *The Vulnerable Text*.

ALDO SCAGLIONE, Professor of Italian and Comparative Literature at the University of North Carolina, is the author of several works including *Nature and Love in the Late Middle Ages* and *Ars grammatica*, and is the editor of Boiardo's *Orlando innamorato*.

VICTORIA KAHN, a member of the English department at Bennington College, is the author of *Rhetoric, Prudence and Skepticism in the Renaissance* and several articles including "Giovanni Pontano's Rhetoric of Prudence" and "The Rhetoric of Faith and the Use of Usage in Lorenzo Valla's *De libero arbitrio*."

Bibliography

Baron, Hans. "The Evolution of Petrarch's Thought: Reflections on the State of Petrarchan Studies" and "Petrarch's *Secretum*: Was It Revised—and Why?" In *From Petrarch to Leonardo Bruni: Studies in Humanistic and Political Literature*, 7–104. Chicago: University of Chicago Press, 1968.

Bergin, Thomas G., and Alice S. Wilson. Introduction to *Petrarch's* Africa. New Haven: Yale University Press, 1977.

Bernardo, Aldo S. *Petrarch, Laura and the* Triumphs. Albany: State University of New York Press, 1974.

Bernardo, Aldo S., and Anthony L. Pellegrini, eds. *Dante, Petrarch and Boccaccio: Studies in the Italian Trecento in Honor of Charles Singleton*. Binghamton: Center for Medieval and Early Renaissance Studies, State University of New York Press, 1983.

Billanovich, Giuseppe. "Petrarch and the Textual Tradition of Livy." *Journal of the Warburg and Courtauld Institutes* 14 (1951): 137–208.

Bishop, Morris. *Petrarch and His World*. Bloomington: Indiana University Press, 1963.

Cassirer, Ernst, P. O. Kristeller, and J. H. Randall, Jr., eds. and trans. "Petrarch." In *The Renaissance Philosophy of Man*, 23–143. Chicago: University of Chicago Press, 1948.

Cave, Terence. "The Mimesis of Reading in the Renaissance." In *Mimesis: From Mirror to Method, Augustine to Descartes,* edited by John D. Lyons and Stephen G. Nichols, Jr. Hanover, N.H.: University Press of New England, 1982.

Chiapelli, Carolyn. "The Motif of Confession in Petrarch's 'Mt. Ventoux.' " *MLN* 93 (1978): 131–36.

Corrigan, Beatrice. "Petrarch in English." *Italica* 50 (1973): 400–407.

De Sanctis, Francesco. "Petrarch." In *History of Italian Literature*, vol. 1, translated by Joan Redfern, 264–89. New York: Basic Books, 1959.

Durling, Robert. "Petrarch's 'Giovene donna sotto un verde lauro.' " *MLN* 86 (1971): 1–20.

———, trans. Introduction to *Petrarch's Lyric Poems*. Cambridge: Harvard University Press, 1976.

Dutschke, Dennis. "The Textual Situation and Chronological Assessment of Petrarch's Canzone 23." *Italian Quarterly* 18, no. 69 (1974): 37–69.

Foster, Kenelm, O.P. "Beatrice or Medusa: The Penetential Element in Petrarch's *Canzoniere*." In *Italian Studies Presented to E. R. Vincent*, 41–56. Cambridge, Eng.: Heffer, 1962.

Freccero, John. "Medusa: The Letter and the Spirit." *Yearbook of Italian Studies* (1972): 1–18.

Garin, Eugeneo. "The Origins of Humanism: From Francis Petrarch to Coluccio Salutati." In *Italian Humanism*, translated by P. Munz, 18–37. New York: Harper & Row, 1965.

Greene, Thomas. "The Flexibility of the Self in Renaissance Literature." In *The Disciplines of Criticism*, edited by Peter Demetz, Thomas Greene, and Lowry Nelson, Jr., 241–64. New Haven: Yale University Press, 1968.

Hardison, O. B., Jr. *The Enduring Monument: A Study of the Idea of Praise in Renaissance Literary Theory and Practice*. Chapel Hill: University of North Carolina Press, 1962.

Mommsen, Theodor E. "Petrarchan Studies." In *Medieval and Renaissance Studies*, edited by Eugene E. Rice. Jr., 73–261. Ithaca, N.Y.: Cornell University Press, 1959.

North Carolina Studies in Philology, vol. 72, no. 5 (1975). Special Petrarch issue.

O'Connell, Michael. "Authority and the Truth of Experience in Petrarch's 'Ventoux.' " *Philological Quarterly* 62 (1983): 507–20.

Phelps, Ruth Shepard. *The Earlier and Later Forms of Petrarch's* Canzoniere. Chicago: University of Chicago Press, 1925.

Quasimodo, Salvatore. "Petrarch and the Sentiment of Solitude." In *The Poet and the Politician and Other Essays*, translated by Thomas Bergin and Sergio Pacifici, 60–66. Carbondale: Southern Illinois University Press, 1964.

Quinones, Ricardo J. "Petrarch." In *The Renaissance Discovery of Time*, 106–71. Cambridge: Harvard University Press, 1972.

Rigolot, François. "Nature and Function of Paranomasia in the *Canzoniere*." *Italian Quarterly* 18, no. 69 (1974): 29–36.

Robinson, J. H., and H. W. Rolfe. *Petrarch: The First Modern Scholar and Man of Letters*. 2d ed. New York: Putnam, 1914.

Roche, Thomas P. "The Calandrical Structure of Petrarch's *Canzoniere*." *Studies in Philology* 71 (1974): 152–72.

Seigel, Jerrold E. "Ideals of Eloquence and Silence in Petrarch." In *Rhetoric and Philosophy in Renaissance Humanism*, 31–62. Princeton: Princeton University Press, 1968.

Smarr, Janet. "Petrarch: A Vergil without a Rome." In *Rome and the Renaissance: The City and the Myth*, edited by P. A. Ramsey, 133–40. Binghamton: Center for Medieval and Early Renaissance Studies, State University of New York Press, 1982.

Sturm-Maddox, Sarah. *Petrarch's Metamorphoses*. Columbia: University of Missouri Press, 1985.

Tatham, Edward H. R. *Francesco Petrarca, the First Modern Man of Letters, His Life and Correspondence: A Study of the Early Fourteenth Century (1304–1347)*. 2 vols. London: Sheldon, 1925–26.

Tilden, Jill. "Spiritual Conflict in Petrarch's *Canzoniere*." In *Beitrage zu Werk und Wirkung*, edited by F. Schalk, 287–319. Frankfurt: Vittorio Klostermann, 1975.

Trinkhaus, Charles. *The Poet as Philosopher*. New Haven: Yale University Press, 1979.

Ullman, B. L. "Petrarch's Favorite Books." In *Studies in the Italian Renaissance*, 113–33. Rome: Edizioni di storia e letteratura, 1955.

Vickers, Nancy J. "The Body Re-membered: Petrarchan Lyrics and the Strategies of Description." In *Mimesis: From Mirror to Method, Augustine to Descartes*, edited by John D. Lyons and Stephen G. Nichols, Jr., 100–109. Hanover, N.H.: University Press of New England for Dartmouth College, 1982.

Watkins, Renee Neu. "Petrarch and the Black Death: From Fear to Monuments." *Studies in the Renaissance* 19 (1972): 196–223.

Wilkins, E. H. *The Invention of the Sonnet, and Other Studies in Italian Literature.* Rome: Edizioni di storia e letteratura, 1959.

———. *Life of Petrarch.* Chicago: University of Chicago Press, 1961.

———. *The Making of the* Canzoniere *and Other Petrarchan Studies.* Rome: Edizioni di storia e letteratura, 1951.

———. *Studies in the Life and Works of Petrarch.* Cambridge: Medieval Academy of America, 1955.

Acknowledgments

"Scipio vs. Laura: 'From Young Leaves to Garlands' " by Aldo S. Bernardo from *Petrarch, Scipio and the "Africa": The Birth of Humanism's Dream* by Aldo S. Bernardo, © 1962 by the Johns Hopkins University Press, Baltimore/London. Reprinted by permission of the Johns Hopkins University Press. All translations of the *Canzoniere* are from Robert Durling, *Petrarch's Lyric Poems*. Cambridge: Harvard University Press, 1976.

"The Ascent of Mt. Ventoux and the Crisis of Allegory" by Robert M. Durling from *Italian Quarterly* 18, no. 69 (Summer 1974), © 1974 by the University of Massachusetts. Reprinted by permission.

"The Fig Tree and the Laurel: Petrarch's Poetics" by John Freccero from *Literary Theory/Renaissance Texts*, edited by Patricia Parker and David Quint, © 1986 by the Johns Hopkins University Press, Baltimore/London. Reprinted by permission. This essay originally appeared in *Diacritics* 5, no. 1 (Spring 1975), © 1975 by Diacritics, Inc. Reprinted by permission.

"The *Canzoniere* and the Language of the Self" by Giusseppe Mazzotta from *Studies in Philology* 75, no. 3 (Summer 1978), © 1978 by the University of North Carolina Press. Reprinted by permission of the author and the University of North Carolina Press. All translations of Petrarch's *Rime* are by Robert Durling from *Petrarch's Lyric Poems*. Cambridge: Harvard University Press, 1976.

"Negative Stylistics: A Reading of the *Trionfi*" (originally entitled "Negative Stylistics: A Reading of Petrarch's *Trionfi*") by Marguerite Waller from *Petrarch's Poetics and Literary History* by Marguerite Waller, © 1980 by the University of Massachusetts Press. Reprinted by permission of the University of Massachusetts Press, Amherst.

"Petrarch and the Humanist Hermeneutic" by Thomas M. Greene from *The Light in Troy: Imitation and Discovery in Renaissance Poetry* by Thomas M. Greene, © 1982 by Yale University. Reprinted by permission of Yale University Press.

"Classical Heritage and Petrarchan Self-Consciousness in the Literary Emergence of the Interior 'I' " by Aldo Scaglione from *Altro Polo: The Classical Continuum*

167

Index

169

Modern Critical Views